330

A-LEVEL YEAR 2

STUDENT GUIDE

AQA

Economics

The national and international economy

Ray Powell and James Powell

D0315963

Hodder Education, an Hachette UK company, Blenheim Court, George Street, Banbury, Oxfordshire OX16 5BH

Orders

Bookpoint Ltd, 130 Park Drive, Milton Park, Abingdon, Oxfordshire OX14 4SB

tel: 01235 827827

fax: 01235 400401

e-mail: education@bookpoint.co.uk

Lines are open 9.00 a.m.–5.00 p.m., Monday to Saturday, with a 24-hour message answering service. You can also order through the Hodder Education website: www.hoddereducation.co.uk

© Ray Powell and James Powell 2016

ISBN 978-1-4718-5770-6

First printed 2016

Impression number 5 4 3 2 1

Year 2020 2019 2018 2017 2016

This Guide has been written specifically to support students preparing for the AQA A-level Economics examinations. The content has been neither approved nor endorsed by AQA and remains the sole responsibility of the authors.

Typeset by Integra Software Services Pvt. Ltd., Pondicherry, India

Cover photo: gui yong nian/Fotolia

Printed in Italy

Hachette UK's policy is to use papers that are natural, renewable and recyclable products and made from wood grown in sustainable forests. The logging and manufacturing processes are expected to conform to the environmental regulations of the country of origin.

Contents

∎Getting the most from this book

Exam tips

Advice on key points in the text to help you learn and recall content, avoid pitfalls, and polish your exam technique in order to boost your grade.

Knowledge check

Rapid-fire questions throughout the Content Guidance section to check your understanding.

Knowledge check answers

1 Turn to the back of the book for the Knowledge check answers.

Summaries

■ Each core topic is rounded off by a bullet-list summary for quick-check reference of what you need to know.

Questions & Answers

finished clothing increased. In 2008 the value of exports was £3,500m and by 2013 it had risen to £5,500m, an increase of 57%. This suggests that UK clothing firms have benefited from the long-term increases that have taken place in world and UK trade in clothing and footwear since 1993. In the 20 years between 1993 and 2013 trade grew in every year, except 2009, and total trade increased by 225%.

Overall the data suggest that both UK consumers and producers have benefited from free trade since 2008.

ⓔ 10/10 marks awarded. An excellent answer, which does exactly what is required by the wording of the question, namely to discuss to what extent, if at all, the data support the view that both UK clothing manufacturers and consumers benefit from free trade in clothing and footwear. The student makes good use of the data in Extract C and includes and explains an appropriate diagram, even though the question does not require the use of a diagram. The answer reaches the top of Level 3 (8–10 marks) in the mark scheme, providing a good response that is well organised and makes effective use of the data in Extract C.

(32) Lines 2–5 of Extract B state 'international specialisation and complete free trade, undertaken in accordance with the principle of comparative advantage, benefits all the countries involved.'

Explain how the theory of comparative advantage is used by economists to justify free trade and to oppose import controls and other forms of protectionism.   [15 marks]

ⓔ This question requires explanation and analysis but not evaluation.

Student answer

(32) Comparative advantage is an economic model devised in the early nineteenth century by the classical economist David Ricardo that built upon the absolute advantage model of another classical economist, Adam Smith. Absolute advantage shows that if countries are better at producing a good than another country they should specialise in what they do best and then trade their surpluses. Comparative advantage is a more sophisticated model because it shows that as long as opportunity costs differ, countries can benefit from partial specialisation. Both trade models advocate free trade on the grounds that if countries specialise and trade then they can benefit from significant output gains. Economists assume that if countries are increasing the level of production then they are producing more consumer and capital goods. This will in turn lead to faster levels of economic growth and higher living standards. It is for this reason that Extract A favours free trade and resists protectionist trade barriers.

Trade barriers are introduced by a government with the aim of protecting domestic firms from cheaper international competition. As Extract B says, countries favour free trade when they 'face little or no competition' but once competition emerges they impose import controls to 'pull up the drawbridge'.

106 AQA Economics

Exam-style questions

Commentary on the questions

Tips on what you need to do to gain full marks, indicated by the icon ⓔ

Sample student answers

Practise the questions, then look at the student answers that follow.

Commentary on sample student answers

Read the comments (preceded by the icon ⓔ) showing how many marks each answer would be awarded in the exam and exactly where marks are gained or lost.

■ About this book

The aim of this guide is to prepare students for the AQA A-level Paper 2 'The national and international economy' examination and for the macroeconomic parts of AQA A-level Paper 3. All the topics explained in this book could be examined in the A-level Paper 3, which is a synoptic paper testing the whole of the A-level specification.

Content Guidance

The Content Guidance section of this book covers six macroeconomic topics in the order in which they appear in the AQA A-level 'The national and international economy' specification, starting from 'The measurement of macroeconomic performance' and finishing with 'The international economy'. Start off by reading this section, topic by topic, before proceeding to the Questions & Answers section of the guide. Alternatively, you may decide to read a particular topic and then the corresponding part of the Questions & Answers section.

Questions & Answers

You should read the Questions & Answers section of the guide either after reading all six specification topics in the Content Guidance section, or bit by bit, having revised a selected topic on a particular part of the specification. This final section of the guide includes example of all the forms of assessment in the A-level economics examination. These are multiple-choice questions (MCQs), data-response questions (DRQs), essay questions (EQs) and finally an extended investigation/case study question (IQ).

This guide should be used as a supplement to other resources, such as class notes, the *AQA A-level Economics for A-level Year 2* textbook, the *Economic Review* magazine and *AS/A-level Economics My Revision Notes* (all published by Philip Allan for Hodder Education). As this guide contains summaries rather than in-depth coverage of all the topics in the specification, you should not use the guide as your sole learning resource during the main part of the course. However, you may well decide to use the guide as the key resource in your revision programme. You are strongly advised to make full use of the Questions & Answers section, especially in the revision period when you should be concentrating on improving your examination skills.

Content Guidance

■ Introduction to the specification

The AQA A-level specification for 'The national and international economy' contains the following six sections:

- 4.2.1 The measurement of macroeconomic performance
- 4.2.2 How the macroeconomy works: the circular flow of income, aggregate demand/aggregate supply analysis and related concepts
- 4.2.3 Economic performance
- 4.2.4 Financial markets and monetary policy
- 4.2.5 Fiscal policy and supply-side policies
- 4.2.6 The international economy

Specification sections 4.2.1, 4.2.2 and 4.2.3 are also covered in *Student Guide 2: The national economy in a global context*. Similarly, monetary policy, fiscal policy and supply-side policies, covered in sections 4.2.4 and 4.2.5 in this guide, are covered in less detail in *Student Guide 2* in the section on macroeconomic policy. Apart from brief coverage of the current account of the balance of payments in sections 3.2.1 and 3.2.3 of *Student Guide 2*, the coverage of section 4.2.6 'The international economy' is new to this guide.

4.2.1 The measurement of macroeconomic performance

The measurement of macroeconomic performance is the first in the list of topics in both the A-level ('The national and international economy') and the AS ('The national economy in a global context') specifications.

With one exception, the content of A-level specification section 4.2.1 is identical to section 3.2.1 in the AS specification. For this reason, the coverage in this guide of the subsections 4.2.1.1 'The objectives of government economic policy', 4.2.1.2 'Macroeconomic indicators' and 4.2.1.3 'Uses of index numbers' mixes short summaries of specification content with page references to *Student Guide 2: The national economy in a global context*.

The one exception is the A-level specification section 4.2.2.4 'Uses of national income data'. This topic is explained in more detail in this guide to reflect the fact that it is not covered in *Student Guide 2*.

4.2.2 How the macroeconomy works: the circular flow of income, aggregate demand/ aggregate supply analysis and related concepts

This is the theoretical core of the specification, focusing on two interrelated macroeconomic models of the economy: the aggregate demand/aggregate supply (*AD/AS*) model and the circular flow model.

AD curves and AS curves are brought together in the aggregate demand/aggregate supply (AD/AS) model of the macroeconomy. Macroeconomic equilibrium occurs at the level of real national income or output at which total planned spending equals the quantity of goods and services firms are willing and able to supply, i.e. at the level of output at which $AD = AS$.

4.2.3 Economic performance

The performance of the national economy can be measured by the extent to which the government's macroeconomic policy objectives have been achieved and by the extent to which these objectives can continue to be achieved in future years.

If all the main policy objectives, such as economic growth, low unemployment, control of inflation and a satisfactory balance of payments on current account, could be achieved simultaneously all the time, the economic problem would largely disappear. However, it is very difficult and perhaps impossible to achieve this. Very often, the more successful a government is at hitting one particular objective, the poorer is its performance with regard to one or more of the other objectives. Governments are often faced with policy conflicts, which they may try to resolve by trading off between competing objectives.

4.2.4 Financial markets and monetary policy

The efficiency and effectiveness of financial markets influence both the short-run and the long-run growth of developed countries such as the UK. As well as understanding some of the principal financial markets, namely money markets, capital markets and foreign exchange markets, it is necessary to appreciate the role of monetary policy in managing the economy, and to evaluate the strengths and limitations of monetary policy measures. In order to do this, it is first necessary to understand that bank deposits rather than cash form the main part of the money supply or stock of money in the economy, and how commercial banks create bank deposits and credit.

4.2.5 Fiscal policy and supply-side policies

With regard to fiscal policy, the specification states that students should be able to assess the economic significance of changes in the level and distribution of both public expenditure and taxation.

Students should be aware of issues relating to the budget balance and be able to evaluate the possible economic consequences of a government running a budget deficit or budget surplus. They should be able to assess the impact of measures used to rebalance the budget. It is important to distinguish between demand-side and supply-side fiscal policy and to appreciate the fact that supply-side fiscal policy is arguably the most important element of supply-side policies in general. It is important to understand the role of the Office for Budgetary Responsibility (OBR) and the links between the OBR and the Treasury.

4.2.6 The international economy

Globalisation requires understanding of its various facets, and its effects, for good and for bad, on trade and the location decisions of multinational corporations. It is important to understand the benefits of international trade and the principle of comparative advantage, together with the possible costs of international specialisation. Theories of protectionism can be put into a European context related to the European Union (EU) as a customs union. Coverage of trade theory includes understanding patterns of trade between the UK and the rest of the world including with the EU, post Brexit.

Some knowledge of the financial account of the balance of payments is needed, covering the nature and significance of both short-term and long-term international capital flows. It is important to link current account deficits and surpluses in the balance of payments, together with capital flows, to the exchange rate. Knowledge of both freely floating and fixed exchange rates is required, together with their links to interest rates and monetary policy and to domestic macroeconomic policy and conflicts. Related to the EU are the advantages and disadvantages of the euro.

It is important to appreciate the links between development issues and other parts of the specification, such as globalisation, trade and the determinants of economic growth and inequality. Market-based strategies and interventionist strategies for promoting growth and development should be compared.

■ 4.2.1 The measurement of macroeconomic performance

These notes relate to AQA specification section 4.2.1 and prepare you to answer examination questions on:

- the objectives of government economic policy
- macroeconomic indicators
- uses of index numbers
- uses of national income data

Essential information

The objectives of government economic policy

A **policy objective** is a target or goal that a government wishes to achieve or 'hit'. Since the Second World War, governments in mixed economies such as the UK have generally had the same broad range of objectives. These are to:

- achieve **economic growth** and improve living standards and levels of economic welfare
- create and maintain **full employment** or low unemployment
- limit or control **inflation**, or achieve some measure of price stability
- attain a satisfactory **balance of payments**, usually defined as the avoidance of an external deficit which might create an **exchange rate** crisis

You should be aware that the importance attached to the different objectives changes over time. For example, in recent decades, control of inflation was the most important macroeconomic objective in the UK. However, following the onset of recession in 2008, successive UK governments have generally replaced the control of inflation with

Policy objective A target or goal which the government's economic policy-makers wish to achieve.

Economic growth The rate of increase in the potential output of an economy.

Full employment The level of employment occurring at the market-clearing real-wage rate, where the number of workers whom employers wish to hire equals the number of workers wanting to work.

Inflation A continuous and persistent rise in the price level and a fall in the value of money.

Balance of payments The record of all money flows or transactions between the residents of a country and the rest of the world in a particular period, usually monthly, quarterly or annually.

Exchange rate The external price of a currency, usually measured against another currency such as the US dollar or the euro.

the economic recovery objectives of achieving falling unemployment and a satisfactory and sustainable rate of economic growth.

The government may also have other macroeconomic policy objectives, such as balancing the budget and achieving an equitable distribution of income. You should also be aware of the possibility of **policy conflict** arising, at least in the short run, when attempting to achieve these objectives.

Over the years, UK macroeconomic policy has been influenced and constrained by four significant conflicts between policy objectives. The main policy conflicts and their associated **policy trade-offs** are:

- between the internal policy objectives of full employment and growth and the external objective of achieving a satisfactory balance of payments (or possibly supporting a particular exchange rate)
- between achieving full employment and controlling inflation
- between increasing the rate of economic growth and achieving a more equal distribution of income and wealth
- between higher living standards now and higher living standards in the future

Not all objectives conflict, however. Some economists believe that, with the 'right' policies, policy conflicts do not occur in the long run — i.e. they are compatible. Most economists agree that these policy conflicts and trade-offs pose considerable problems for governments in the economic short run. However, there is much less agreement about whether they need be significant in the long run — a period extending many years into the future.

Macroeconomic indicators

Whereas a policy objective is a target or goal that a government wishes to 'hit', and a **policy instrument** is a tool used to achieve this end, a **policy indicator** simply provides the government with information about the state of the economy and/or whether current policy is 'on course' to achieve the government's objectives.

Along with other economic indicators, such as surveys of business and consumer confidence and information about new houses being built and summer holidays booked, changes in gross domestic product (GDP), levels of unemployment, the price level and the money supply all provide the government with information about what is happening, and what is likely to happen, in the UK economy.

Uses of index numbers

Changes in real GDP, along with other economic variables, are often expressed in terms of changes in an **index number**. Because index numbers frequently appear in the quantitative data you are expected to interpret in the course of your studies, it is especially important that you build up an understanding of how economic indices are constructed.

Exam tip

Avoid comparing data expressed in index numbers with data expressed in percentages.

Policy conflict When two or more policy objectives cannot be attained at the same time.

Policy trade-off Choosing between policy objectives to achieve a satisfactory combination of, for example, consumption now and consumption in the future.

Knowledge check 1

How has the relative importance of different policy objectives changed in the UK in recent years?

Exam tip

Make sure you understand the difference between a policy conflict and trading off between competing objectives.

Policy instrument A tool or set of tools used to try to achieve one or more policy objectives.

Policy indicator Provides information about the state of the economy.

Index number A number used in an index, such as the consumer prices index, to enable accurate comparisons to be made over time.

Economists frequently use index numbers when making comparisons over periods of time. An index starts in a given year, called the base year, which is given an index number of 100. In later years or months, an increase in the size of the variable causes the index number to rise above 100, while a fall in the size of the variable, compared to the base year, results in the index number falling to below 100. For example, an index number of 108 means an 8% rise from the base year, whereas an index number of 92 means an 8% fall.

There are a number of points to be aware of when interpreting data shown by changes in index numbers:

- Providing you are comparing the index number for one of the years in a data series with the base year index number of 100, the increase in the index number is the same as the percentage increase over the data period you are looking at.
- A change in the index numbers is not the same as a percentage change when a comparison is made with a year other than the base year.
- When comparing data series which are presented in index numbers, *relative* changes in each data series can usually be identified, but not *absolute* changes or the *absolute* levels of the economic variables shown in the data series. (See MCQ 2 in the Questions & Answers section of this guide for explanation of this point.)

Uses of national income data

Economists use the terms national income, national output and national product interchangeably. To produce the flow of national income or output, the economy must possess a stock of physical capital goods (the national capital stock) and a stock of human capital, together with stocks of the other factors of production: land and entrepreneurship.

When national income statistics are used as indicators of economic growth (and economic development), gross domestic product (GDP) or gross national income (GNI) per capita (per head of population) should be used rather than 'raw' GDP or GNI statistics.

It is important for you to understand the uses and limitations of national income data to:

- assess changes in living standards over time
- compare differences in living standards between countries

When discussing whether national income figures provide the best measures of standards of living, economic welfare and economic development, it is useful first to identify three components of economic welfare. These are shown below:

National income The flow of new output produced by the economy in a particular period (e.g. a year).

Economic development Improvement in the economic welfare and standard of living of most or all of the population. Economic growth is one aspect of the process of economic development.

Standards of living How well or how poorly people live in terms of having their needs and wants met.

Economic welfare The satisfaction, pleasure, utility or 'happiness' enjoyed by a person or persons.

$$\text{total economic welfare} = \begin{array}{c}\text{economic welfare derived} \\ \text{from goods and services} \\ \text{purchased in the market} \\ \text{economy}\end{array} + \begin{array}{c}\text{economic welfare derived} \\ \text{from public goods and} \\ \text{merit goods provided} \\ \text{collectively by the state}\end{array} + \begin{array}{c}\text{economic welfare derived from} \\ \text{quality of life factors, including} \\ \text{external benefits minus external} \\ \text{costs and intangibles}\end{array}$$

If used carefully, national income figures can provide a reasonable estimate of economic welfare derived from the first two of these three elements, both of which relate to the direct consumption of material goods and services. However, national income fails to provide a satisfactory indication of how externalities and other quality of life factors affect economic welfare and living standards. Intangible factors, which are the third element in people's living standards, are largely ignored. These intangible factors include the value people place on leisure time and living close to work, and the externalities such as pollution and road congestion generated from the production and consumption of national income, which affect people's welfare and quality of life.

National income also fails to reflect the effect on humankind's ability to produce future income of the resource depletion and environmental degradation resulting from producing current income. This means that national income and GDP do not address the issue of sustainability.

National income statistics underestimate activity because the non-monetised economy (such as housework and DIY) is under-represented, and because activity undertaken illegally in the hidden economy (or black economy) is omitted. Improvements in the quality of goods may also be under-represented in national income statistics.

Indicators such as life expectancy, infant mortality rates and literacy rates can be used to supplement national income per head in order to provide a better indicator of the quality of life enjoyed by people.

You must also understand how, in the context of an exchange rate, a purchasing power parity (PPP) exchange rate is used when making international comparisons of living standards. The purchasing power of a currency refers to the quantity of the currency needed to purchase a common basket of goods and services. Purchasing power parity means equalising the purchasing power of two currencies by taking into account these cost-of-living and price-level differences in the two countries. When making comparisons between countries that use different currencies, it is necessary to convert national income values in the different countries to a common currency. This is done by using PPP exchange rates.

Examination skills

The skills most likely to be tested by data-response and essay questions on *the measurement of macroeconomic performance* at A-level are as follows:

- Knowledge of policy objectives and the differences between objectives, instruments and indicators
- Understanding of how policy objectives have changed in recent decades in the UK
- Calculation and interpretation of index numbers
- Analysis of national income data for the purposes of assessing changes in living standards over time and comparing differences in living standards between countries

Examination questions

Questions on *the measurement of macroeconomic performance* are quite likely to be set as both essay questions and data-response questions in Paper 2. Index numbers and national income statistics are likely to figure in tables of data, line graphs and bar graphs in data-response questions in Paper 2 and in the investigation question in Paper 3. You should expect one multiple-choice question which incorporates index number data in Paper 3. The question will require interpretation of the data and/or a calculation. MCQ 1 in the Questions & Answers section of this guide tests understanding of economic policy objectives, while MCQs 2 and 3 involve interpretation of index number and national income data.

> **Knowledge check 2**
>
> What is the difference between resource depletion and environmental degradation?
>
> ....

> **Exchange rate** The external price of a currency, usually measured against another currency such as the US dollar.

> **Purchasing power parity (PPP) exchange rate** The rate at which the currency of one country would have to be converted into that of another country to buy the same amount of goods and services in each country.

Common examination errors

Commonly made mistakes on *the measurement of macroeconomic performance* include:

- confusing policy objectives and policy instruments
- failure to appreciate how policy objectives have changed in recent years
- lack of appreciation of policy conflicts
- failure to understand the meaning of trading off between policy objectives
- confusing changes in index numbers and changes in percentages
- failure to understand purchasing power parity (PPP) exchange rates

Summary

- The main objectives of government macroeconomic policy are full employment, economic growth, control of inflation, and a satisfactory or sustainable balance of payments on current account.
- The importance attached to the different objectives changes over time.
- Economic data are often presented in the form of index numbers.

- National income concepts such as real GDP per capita must be understood.
- The national income of different countries can be compared using PPP exchange rates.
- It is important not to confuse gross and net, and nominal and real national income (output and product).

■ 4.2.2 How the macroeconomy works: the circular flow of income, aggregate demand/ aggregate supply analysis and related concepts

These notes relate to AQA specification section 4.2.2 and prepare you to answer examination questions on:

- the circular flow of income
- aggregate demand and aggregate supply analysis
- the determinants of aggregate demand
- aggregate demand and the level of economic activity
- the determinants of short-run aggregate supply
- the determinants of long-run aggregate supply

Essential information

The circular flow of income

What national income measures

National income is the flow of new output produced in the economy during a particular period of time, for example a month, a quarter or a year. **Gross domestic product (GDP)** is perhaps the most commonly used measure of national income. GDP is the sum of all goods and services, or the level of output, produced in the economy over a period of time, e.g. one year.

The difference between nominal and real income

Nominal national income (output or product) measures the flow of new output at current prices *before* taking account of inflation or changes in the price level. By contrast, **real national income** (output or product) measures the flow of new output *after* taking account of inflation or changes in the price level.

Real national income as an indicator of economic performance

Indicators of economic performance can be divided into *lead* and *lag* indicators. Lead indicators, such as surveys of consumer and business confidence and investment intentions, provide information about the *future* state of the economy. By contrast, tables showing how real national income has changed over the years are a lag indicator, providing information about past economic growth.

The circular flow of income and the concepts of equilibrium and full employment income

The **circular flow of income**, shown on a circular flow diagram such as Figure 1, can be used to analyse the effects of injections of spending and withdrawals of spending on the national economy. The dashed flow lines in the diagram show the *real* flows occurring in the economy between households and firms. Households supply labour and other factor services in exchange for goods and services produced by the firms. But these real flows generate money flows (or *nominal* flows) of income and spending shown by the solid flow lines.

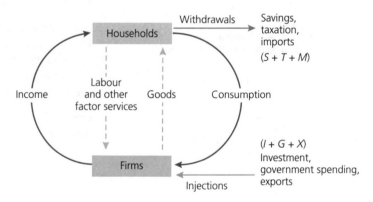

Figure 1 The circular flow of income

Gross domestic product (GDP) The domestically produced part of national income before a deduction is made for the wearing out of capital goods used up in its production.

Nominal national income The flow of new output measured at current prices before taking account of inflation.

Real national income The flow of new output after taking account of inflation.

Circular flow of income In the economy, income received by households from selling labour and other factor services to firms circulates back to the firms when spent by households on goods and services produced by the firms.

Knowledge check 3

Why is it important to distinguish between *real* flows and *money* flows (or *nominal* flows) in the circular flow of income?

The difference between injections into and withdrawals from the circular flow of income

Figure 1 shows three **withdrawals** or leakages of spending out of the circular flow of income. These are **saving**, **taxation** and **imports** $(S + T + M)$. These are shown by the horizontal arrow at the top of the diagram. As well as these three withdrawals of spending, there are three **injections** of spending into the circular flow. These are **investment**, **government spending** and **exports** $(I, G$ and $X)$. The three injections of spending are shown by the horizontal arrow at the bottom of the diagram.

The effects of changes in injections and withdrawals on national income are explained on pages 18 and 19 in *Student Guide 2*, under the heading 'The circular flow of income'.

Aggregate demand and aggregate supply analysis

The **aggregate demand/aggregate supply** (*AD/AS*) model of how the economy's goods market operates, which is illustrated in Figure 2 below, is the main theoretical framework used at A-level for explaining macroeconomic issues. For example, the model is useful for analysing the effect of an increase in aggregate demand on the economy.

> **Aggregate demand** Total planned aggregate spending on real national output. The aggregate demand (*AD*) curve shows total planned aggregate spending at different average price levels.

> **Aggregate supply** Total planned supply of real output by all the producers in the economy.

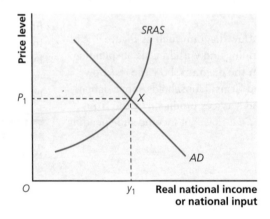

Figure 2 The *AD/AS* model of the economy's goods market

The aggregate demand (*AD*) curve shows the total planned spending of all the economic agents in the economy at different price levels. The *AD* curve slopes downward, showing a greater level of aggregate demand at lower price levels. By contrast, the *AS* curve in Figure 2 slopes upward, showing that all the producers in the economy plan to supply more at higher price levels.

Withdrawals Leakages of spending power out of the circular flow of income into savings, taxation or imports.

Saving Income which is not spent.

Taxation Compulsory levies made by government, which people have to pay.

Imports Goods or services produced in other countries and sold to residents of this country.

Injections Investment spending by firms on capital goods (*I*), government spending (*G*) and overseas spending on the economy's exports (*X*) are injections into the circular flow of income.

Investment Total planned spending on capital goods produced within the economy.

Government spending Total planned spending by the government on real output produced within the economy.

Exports Domestically produced goods or services sold to residents of other countries.

In Figure 2, the level of equilibrium national income occurs at y_1, which is immediately below point X where $AD = AS$. Equilibrium national income is not necessarily the same as the full employment level of national income, which occurs when the 'normal capacity' level of output is produced.

There are in fact two versions of the AS curve, known respectively as the short-run aggregate supply ($SRAS$) curve and the long-run aggregate supply ($LRAS$) curve. We explain these below under the heading 'The factors that affect the short-run and long-run AS curves'.

> Short-run aggregate supply The quantities of real output that businesses plan to produce and sell at different price levels when total productive capacity is fixed but when variable factors of production can be changed.

> Long-run aggregate supply The real output that can be supplied when the economy is on its production possibility frontier (PPF). This is when all the available factors of production are employed and producing at their 'normal capacity' level of output.

The factors that shift the AD curve and the short-run AS curve

If either the AD curve or the AS curve shifts to a new position, equilibrium national income will change. If any of the determinants of aggregate demand change (apart from the price level), the AD curve shifts to the right or left, depending on whether there has been an increase or a decrease in aggregate demand. As we explain under the heading 'The determinants of aggregate demand', a change in any of the components of aggregate demand (consumption, investment, government spending or net export demand) moves the AD curve to a new position.

The position of the $SRAS$ curve is determined by a number of factors, which include firms' costs of production, for example money wage rates and raw material costs, the taxes firms have to pay and changes in labour productivity. If any of these factors change, the $SRAS$ curve shifts to a new position. For example, an increase in business costs shifts the $SRAS$ curve upwards and to the left.

The factors that affect the short-run and long-run AS curves

The $SRAS$ curve must not be confused with the long-run aggregate supply ($LRAS$) curve, which we now explain. The $LRAS$ curve, depicted in Figure 3, shows the maximum level of real output the economy can produce at its production potential, when all the available factors of production are employed and producing at their 'normal capacity' level of output (y_N). In the long run, firms cannot produce more output to meet the increase in aggregate demand, shown by the shift of the AD curve from AD_1 to AD_2. In the short run, firms may be able to produce beyond their long-run sustainable level of output, but the emerging positive output gap will generate inflationary pressures. In this situation, the excess demand for real output is met by an increase in the price level, with the point of macroeconomic equilibrium moving from point X to point Z.

Equilibrium national income The level of real output at which $AD = AS$.

Productivity Output per unit of input. The most common measure is labour productivity, which is output per worker.

Exam tip

Make sure you don't confuse short-run aggregate supply curves and long-run aggregate supply curves.

Positive output gap When the current level of real GDP is above the potential output of the economy.

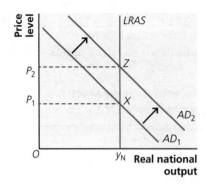

Figure 3 A vertical *LRAS* curve located at the 'normal capacity' level of real output, y_N

In summary, a change in businesses' costs of production shifts the position of an *SRAS* curve, whereas a change in the economy's underlying production potential shifts the position of the *LRAS* curve.

Underlying economic growth is represented by a rightward shift in the long-run AS curve

Underlying economic growth can be illustrated by a movement *along* the trend output line shown in the upper panel of Figure 4. (Actual growth, by contrast, is shown by a movement along the 'wavy' line depicting the **economic cycle** on the same diagram.) Underlying economic growth is also represented by the rightward shift of the *LRAS* curve shown in the lower panel of Figure 4.

Economic cycle Upswing and downswing in aggregate economic activity, usually taking place over 4 to 12 years. Also known as a business cycle or a trade cycle.

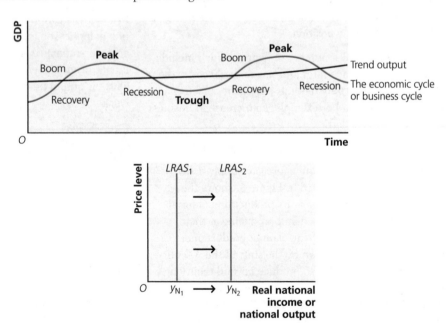

Figure 4 Underlying economic growth in the economy shown by a movement along the trend output line and by a rightward shift of the *LRAS* curve

How to use AD/AS diagrams to illustrate macroeconomic equilibrium

The concept of macroeconomic equilibrium is exactly the same as the concept of the equilibrium level of national income, which was previously illustrated in Figure 2. Figure 5, below, goes one stage further and illustrates the concept in a diagram which incorporates the *LRAS* curve as well as the *SRAS* curve.

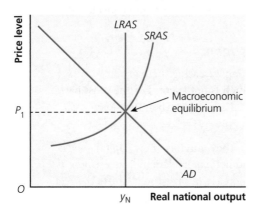

Figure 5 Macroeconomic equilibrium illustrated on a diagram incorporating an *LRAS* curve as well as an *SRAS* curve

How both demand-side and supply-side shocks affect the macroeconomy

An **economic shock** is a sudden unexpected event hitting the economy, disturbing either aggregate demand (a demand shock) or aggregate supply (a supply shock). In some cases, an outside shock may affect both aggregate demand and aggregate supply. Thus, looking at the UK economy, the outbreak of a war in the Middle East, for example, may affect aggregate demand by causing a sudden collapse in consumer and business confidence, and aggregate supply via its effect on the supply and price of crude oil.

The determinants of aggregate demand

As we mentioned earlier, aggregate demand is total planned spending on real national output in the economy. Aggregate demand is the addition of consumption, investment, government spending and net export demand, and is represented by the equation $AD = C + I + G + (X - M)$, where C, I, G, X and M are the symbols used respectively for planned consumption, investment, government spending and net export demand $(X - M)$. These are often called the components of aggregate demand. At this point, you might wish to reread pages 21 to 23 in *Student Guide 2*, to find out more about each of these components of aggregate demand.

If any of the components change, aggregate demand increases or decreases. On a diagram, an increase in aggregate demand is depicted by a rightward shift of the *AD* curve, while a decrease in aggregate demand is represented by a leftward shift of the curve.

Knowledge check 4

Distinguish between *microeconomic* equilibrium and *macroeconomic* equilibrium.

Economic shock An unexpected event hitting the economy. A supply shock such as a natural disaster shifts the *AS* curve, whereas a demand shock, such as collapse in consumer confidence, shifts the *AD* curve.

Content Guidance

The determinants of savings

If we simplify and assume that there are no imports or taxes, saving is simply income which is not consumed. It follows that the determinants of saving are exactly the same as the determinants of consumption, which are explained on page 22 of *Study Guide 2*. In summary, the determinants of saving (and of consumption) are the rate of interest, the level of income, expected future income, wealth, consumer confidence, and the availability of credit.

The difference between saving and investment

Students often confuse saving and investment, wrongly treating them as interchangeable terms. Saving is simply income which is not spent. For the most part, households make savings decisions, though firms can also save when they keep cash reserves which they do not spend.

By contrast, firms make investment decisions when they purchase new capital goods. Along with consumption, government spending and net export demand, investment is one of the components of aggregate demand. An increase in investment shifts the *AD* curve to the right, and, as one of the 'engines' of economic growth, investment also has a supply-side effect, shifting the *LRAS* curve rightward.

The accelerator

Determinants of investment include:

- the state of business confidence and expectations of future profitability of investments undertaken now
- the existence of an 'entrepreneurial culture'
- the rate of interest or cost of borrowing, which affects the cost of obtaining the funds to finance investment projects
- technical progress, which might make existing capital obsolete or out of date, and in need of replacement with 'state-of-the-art' capital
- the relative prices of capital and labour, which influence the choice between capital-intensive and labour-intensive methods of production

Another possible determinant is provided by the **accelerator** theory of investment. The accelerator theory stems from the assumption that firms wish to keep a relatively fixed ratio, known as the capital–output ratio, between the output they are currently producing and their existing stock of fixed capital assets. For example, if four units of capital are needed to produce one new unit of output, the capital–output ratio is 4 to 1. The capital–output ratio *is* the accelerator. To understand why the theory is called the accelerator theory, consider the following:

Accelerator Investment in new capital goods is induced by a change in the rate of growth of national income or aggregate demand.

- If output grows by a constant amount each year, firms invest in exactly the same amount of new capital each year to enlarge their capital stock, so as to maintain the desired capital–output ratio. From year to year, the level of investment is therefore constant.
- If the rate of growth of output *accelerates, investment also increases* as firms take action to enlarge the stock of capital to a level sufficient to maintain the desired capital–output ratio.
- Conversely, when the rate of growth of output *decelerates*, investment declines.

As firms adjust their stocks of capital to maintain the capital–output ratio at 4 to 1, relatively slight changes in the rate of growth of income or output cause large absolute rises and falls in investment.

Aggregate demand and the level of economic activity

The multiplier process and an explanation of why an initial change in expenditure may lead to a larger impact on national income

Whereas the accelerator measures the relationship between a change in national income or output and the resulting change in the level of investment, the investment multiplier measures the relationship between a change in investment and the resulting change in national income or output.

Besides the investment multiplier, there is a government spending multiplier, a tax multiplier, an export multiplier and an import multiplier. Taken together, the government spending and tax multipliers are known as fiscal policy multipliers. Likewise, the export and import multipliers are foreign trade multipliers.

The multiplier process, which is essentially dynamic, taking place over time, resembles ripples spreading over a pond after a stone has been thrown in the water. Figure 6 illustrates the ripple effect, through which the eventual change in national income is larger than (a multiple of) the initial change in aggregate demand which started the process. The figure shows the government spending multiplier.

Multiplier The relationship between a change in aggregate demand and the resulting, usually larger, change in national income.

Fiscal policy The use of government spending and taxation to try to achieve the government's policy objectives.

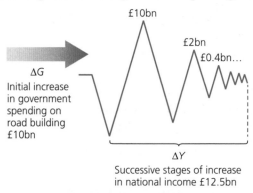

Figure 6 The multiplier process

The formula you need to know for calculating the value of the multiplier is:

$$k = \frac{1}{1 - MPC}$$

where k is the multiplier and MPC is the marginal propensity to consume.

The MPC is the fraction of any increase in income which people plan to spend on the consumption of domestically produced goods, after allowing for the fraction of the increase in income which they pay in taxation to the government, and the fraction spent on imported goods. In Figure 6 we have assumed that people, on average, plan to spend 20p of an income increase of £1 on consumption. This means that the MPC is 0.2, and that at each stage of the multiplier process 20% of income is spent on consumption. In Figure 6, assuming an initial change in government spending of £10 billion, we have numbered the first three stages (£10bn, £2bn and £0.4bn), but adding

Marginal propensity to consume (MPC) The fraction of an increase in disposable income (income after tax) that people plan to spend on domestically produced consumer goods.

on the subsequent stages, national income eventually increases to £12.5 billion. In this example, the size of the multiplier is 1.25.

How the size of the marginal propensity to consume determines the magnitude of the multiplier effect

If the *MPC* is 0.5 rather than 0.2, the multiplier is 1 divided by 0.5, which is +2. Thus the larger the size of the *MPC*, the bigger the multiplier. However, economists generally assume the multiplier in the UK today is fairly close to +1.

Knowledge check 5

Distinguish between the multiplier and the accelerator.

The determinants of short-run aggregate supply

The price level and production costs are the main determinants of the short-run aggregate supply

Although the average price level and production costs both affect short-run aggregate supply, they do so in different ways. Changes in the price level lead to movements *along* the SRAS curve, but not to *shifts* in the curve. As we explained earlier, costs of production such as wage costs are the main determinants of the *position* of the SRAS curve. If any of these costs change, the SRAS curve shifts either upward or downward.

The determinants of long-run aggregate supply

The main determinants of the position of the *LRAS* curve are:
- the state of technical progress
- the quantities of capital and labour and other factors of production in the economy
- the mobility of factors of production, particularly labour
- the productivity of the factors of production, particularly labour productivity
- people's attitudes to hard work
- personal enterprise, particularly among entrepreneurs
- the existence of appropriate economic incentives such as financial rewards for risk-taking

Also important is the institutional structure of the economy, involving such factors as the rule of law and the efficiency of the banking system.

The position of the vertical long-run AS curve represents the normal capacity level of output of the economy

The *LRAS* curve is located at the 'normal capacity' level of output, which is the level of output at which the full production potential of the economy is being used. To put it another way, it is the maximum sustainable level of output that the economy can produce when the economy is on its production possibility frontier. 'Normal capacity' is not quite the same as 'full capacity'. Even when producing at 'normal capacity', the economy may still be capable of temporarily producing a higher level of real output in the 'boom' phase of the economic cycle.

The Keynesian AS curve

Figure 7 illustrates an inverted L-shaped *AS* curve, based on the explanation put forward by John Maynard Keynes of the Great Depression in the UK and US economies in the 1930s. Keynes argued that a depressed economy can settle into an under-full employment equilibrium, shown, for example, by point A on the horizontal section of the AS curve. At point A, the level of real national output is y_1.

Keynes believed that without purposeful intervention by the government, an economy could display more or less permanent demand deficiency. Market forces would fail to adjust automatically and achieve full employment.

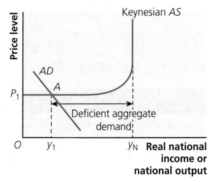

Figure 7 The Keynesian AS curve

If the government could shift AD to the right along the horizontal section of the AS curve (mainly through expansionary fiscal policy), the existence of huge amounts of spare capacity would lead, in Keynes's view, to a growth in real output (and employment), without an increase in the price level. Eventually, when 'normal capacity' is reached, the AS curve becomes vertical for the same reasons that the 'free-market' curve is vertical.

Examination skills

The skills most likely to be tested by data-response and essay questions on *how the macroeconomy works: the circular flow of income, aggregate demand/aggregate supply analysis and related concepts* are as follows:

- Drawing and accurately labelling circular flow and AD/AS diagrams
- Understanding the nature of aggregate demand and aggregate supply
- Using the accelerator and multiplier concepts to explain changes in national income
- Applying marginal analysis to understanding the multiplier process
- Understanding both demand-side and supply-side aspects of AD/AS analysis

Examination questions

The circular flow and aggregate demand/aggregate supply (AD/AS) macroeconomic models provide the main theoretical frameworks that you are expected to apply when analysing and evaluating macroeconomic problems and government policies. The AD/AS model can be used for analysing economic growth, employment and unemployment, inflation, and both demand-side and supply-side economic policy. MCQs 3, 4 and 5 are respectively on changes in national income, the accelerator and the multiplier.

Common examination errors

Commonly made mistakes on *how the macroeconomy works: the circular flow of income, aggregate demand/aggregate supply analysis and related concepts* include:

- incorrect labelling of both circular flow and *AD/AS* diagrams
- confusing macroeconomic *AD* and *AS* curves with microeconomic demand and supply analysis
- wasting time deriving *AD* or *AS* curves, instead of applying them to analyse the issue posed by the question
- failing to relate *AD/AS* diagrams to demand-side and supply-side economic policy

Summary

- National income is the flow of new output produced in the economy during a particular period of time.
- A circular flow diagram can be used to analyse the effects of injections of spending and withdrawals of spending on the national economy.
- In the *AD/AS* model, it is important to distinguish between short-run and long-run aggregate supply.
- If either the *AD* curve or the *AS* curve shifts to a new position, equilibrium national income will change.
- Macroeconomic equilibrium is shown in an *AD/AS* diagram as the level of real national income at which *AD = AS*.

- Aggregate demand = consumption + investment + government spending + exports (net of imports).
- It is important to avoid confusing the multiplier with the accelerator.
- The marginal propensity to consume (*MPC*) is the fraction of an increase in disposable income (income after tax) that people plan to spend on domestically produced consumer goods.
- The position of the *SRAS* curve is largely determined by costs of production, whereas the position of the vertical *LRAS* curve, located at the 'normal capacity' level of output, is determined by technology, productivity, attitudes, enterprise, factor mobility and economic incentives.

4.2.3 Economic performance

These notes relate to AQA specification section 4.2.3 and prepare you to answer examination questions on:

- economic growth and the economic cycle
- employment and unemployment
- inflation and deflation
- possible conflicts between macroeconomic policy objectives

Essential information

Economic growth and the economic cycle

The difference between short-run and long-run growth

Economic growth is defined as the increase in the potential level of real output the economy can produce over a period of time, such as a year. Strictly, this is long-run economic growth and is not the same as short-run economic growth, which occurs when unused capacity is brought into production in the economy. Figure 8 uses the shifts in the economy's *SRAS* and *LRAS* curves to illustrate long-run economic growth. Both forms of growth can also be shown on a production possibility frontier diagram, such as that included in MCQ 7 in the Questions & Answers section of this guide.

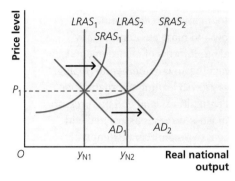

Figure 8 Long-run economic growth illustrated in an *AD/AS* diagram

Short-run economic growth or economic recovery, which can be brought about by an increase in aggregate demand, can continue until 'normal capacity' is reached, for example at y_{N1} in Figure 8. The economy is now producing at its production potential, but by shifting the *LRAS* curve to the right from $LRAS_1$ to $LRAS_2$, long-run growth increases potential output to y_{N2}.

Demand-side and supply-side determinants of short-run growth of real national income, and the long-run trend rate of economic growth

Whereas the determinants of short-run economic growth lie in the demand side of the economy (through an increase in aggregate demand, which absorbs the spare capacity in the economy), long-run economic growth is brought about by changes in the economy's supply side. However, aggregate demand still plays a role in bringing about long-run economic growth. For there to be just sufficient demand in the economy to absorb the extra real output enabled by the rightward shift of the *LRAS* curve shown in Figure 8, aggregate demand must increase to match the increase in aggregate supply.

The costs and benefits of economic growth

Economic growth increases standards of living and people's welfare and life expectancy, and provides the means to reduce disease. It provides a route out of poverty for much of the world's population. Economic growth produces a 'fiscal dividend', namely the tax revenues that growth generates. Tax revenues can be used to correct market failures and to provide infrastructure, thereby increasing the economic welfare of the whole community.

For a particular country, economic growth can generate a 'virtuous circle' of greater business confidence, increased investment in state-of-the-art technology, greater international competitiveness, higher profits, even more growth, and so on.

On the cost side, economic growth uses up finite resources such as oil and minerals that cannot be replaced. Growth can also destroy local cultures and communities and widen inequalities in the distribution of income and wealth. In its early phases, economic growth leads to a rapid growth in population and demographic pressures on resources.

Exam tip

Learn at least two costs and two benefits of economic growth that you could quote in an exam answer.

The impact of growth on individuals, the economy and the environment

We have mentioned how growth can affect the economy. The growth process may lead to more civilised communities, who take action to improve the environment where they live, and also globally. Growth provides new and more environmentally friendly technologies, but it also leads to pollution and other forms of environmental degradation. This may lead to the Earth eventually reaching an environmental tipping point, beyond which it cannot recover. A part of this is growth leading to urbanisation and the spread of huge cities, which swallow up good agricultural land and put pressure on water resources. And although growth greatly diminishes diseases associated with malnutrition such as scurvy and rickets, it replaces them to a significant extent with problems brought about by higher incomes, such as diabetes and obesity.

The economic cycle

While long-run economic growth can be depicted as a movement along the economy's trend output line, short-run economic growth reflects the different phases of the economic cycle. If you refer back to the upper panel of Figure 4 on page 16, you will see an economic cycle and its various phases: recovery, boom and the downswing or recessionary phase.

An economic cycle is usually measured by changes in real output of GDP, though an employment and unemployment cycle is often identified. Variations in the rate of inflation and investment also provide indicators of cyclical fluctuations in economic growth.

The difference between positive and negative output gaps

Output gaps, which are illustrated in Figure 9, are also features of economic cycles. If the economy's *actual* level of output were always to equal trend output, there would be no output gaps, nor indeed economic cycles. Output gaps occur when the level of actual real output in the economy is greater or lower than the trend output level at a particular point in time. When actual output is above trend output, there is a positive output gap. Similarly, when actual output is below trend output, there is a **negative output gap**.

Output gap Measured by the difference between trend output and actual output.

Negative output gap When the current level of real GDP is below the potential output of the economy.

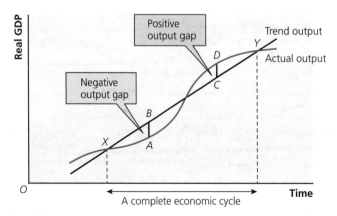

Figure 9 Positive and negative output gaps and the economic cycle

Knowledge check 6

Illustrate positive and negative output gaps on an *AD/AS* diagram.

The causes of changes in the various phases of the economic cycle, including both global and domestic demand-side and supply-side shocks

Economic cycles, which are usually between 4 and 12 years long, are caused primarily by fluctuations in aggregate demand (i.e. by shifts to the left and right of the *AD* curve). There are a number of different theories of the economic cycle and it is advisable to learn at least two theories in a little depth.

One theory is that rapid growth produces a speculative bubble in asset prices (e.g. housing and/or shares), which rise far above the assets' real value. The bubble bursts, destroying consumer and/or business confidence. People stop spending and the economy slows down, perhaps falling into recession (defined in the UK as negative economic growth for 6 months or more).

Second, there is the political business cycle theory. UK governments, which are elected every 5 years, may try to engineer a pre-election boom (to buy votes) and then deflate or contract the economy immediately after the election — until the next pre-election boom. There is also the possibility that random demand shocks (and sometimes supply shocks) throw the economy off course.

Employment and unemployment

The main UK measures of unemployment

There are two measures of unemployment in the UK. These are the **claimant count** and the **Labour Force Survey (LFS)** measure. The claimant count measures the number of people claiming unemployment-related government benefits such as the Universal Credit, which incorporates the old job seeker's allowance (JSA). By contrast, the LFS is a quarterly survey of 60,000 households, which counts people as unemployed if they are actively seeking work and have not had a job during the week in question.

The concepts of voluntary and involuntary unemployment

Voluntary unemployment occurs when workers choose to remain unemployed and refuse job offers at current market wage rates. By contrast, there is **involuntary unemployment** when workers are willing to work at current market wage rates but there are no jobs available. When there is cyclical unemployment (see below), deficient aggregate demand means that much unemployment is involuntary.

Seasonal, frictional, structural and cyclical unemployment

In a dynamic economy, change takes place constantly, with some industries declining and others growing. As new products are developed and demand and cost conditions change, firms demand more of some labour skills while the demand for other types of labour declines.

- **Frictional unemployment** results from frictions in the labour market that create a delay or time-lag during which a worker is unemployed when moving from one job to another.

Exam tip

Learn at least two examples of demand-side and supply-side economic shocks that you could quote in an exam answer.

Claimant count The method of measuring unemployment according to those people who are claiming unemployment-related benefits.

Labour Force Survey (LFS) Quarterly sample survey of households in the UK. Its purpose is to provide information on the UK labour market.

Voluntary unemployment Workers choose to remain unemployed when jobs are available.

Involuntary unemployment Workers are forced into unemployment because jobs are unavailable.

Frictional unemployment Caused in the short term when a worker switches between jobs.

- **Structural unemployment** results from the structural decline of industries unable to compete or adapt in the face of either changing demand and new products, or changing ways of producing existing products and the emergence of more efficient competitors in other countries.
- **Seasonal unemployment**, which results from seasonal fluctuations in demand for certain types of workers, is a fairly trivial source of unemployment — except for those affected.
- Economists generally agree that temporary unemployment (called **cyclical unemployment**) may be caused by a lack of demand in the downswing of the economic cycle. However, Keynes went further, arguing that the economy could settle into an under-full employment equilibrium caused by a continuing lack of effective aggregate demand.

For a fuller account of these types of unemployment, reread pages 31 to 34 in *Student Guide 2*.

How employment and unemployment may be determined by both demand-side and supply-side factors

In the previous section, we suggested that structural unemployment, and perhaps frictional unemployment, are caused by supply-side factors operating within the economy, but that cyclical unemployment and also seasonal unemployment are caused by demand-side factors.

Figure 10 shows how cyclical unemployment occurs — and also how, according to the anti-Keynesian view, it might be corrected by the operation of free-market forces. In the diagram, the economy is initially producing at point X, where the aggregate demand curve AD_1 intersects both the $SRAS$ curve, $SRAS_1$, and the $LRAS$ curve. This means that the economy is producing the 'normal capacity' level of output y_N. A significant fall in aggregate demand, caused, for example, by a collapse of consumer and business confidence, then shifts the AD curve inward from AD_1 to AD_2. Real output falls to y_2, which is considerably below y_N. Cyclical unemployment occurs because fewer workers are needed to produce the level of output y_2 than y_N.

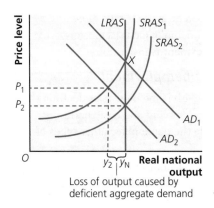

Figure 10 Cyclical unemployment explained by output falling below its 'normal capacity' level

Structural unemployment Long-term unemployment occurring due to a mismatch of skills when some industries are declining, even though other industries may be growing.

Seasonal unemployment Arises in different seasons of the year, caused by factors such as the weather and the end of the Christmas shopping period.

Cyclical unemployment Occurs in the downswing of the economic cycle, caused by a lack of aggregate demand in the economy. Also known as demand-deficient unemployment.

Exam tip

Make sure you can explain unemployment in terms of its demand-side and its supply-side causes.

In the Keynesian view, a 'sticky' wage rate means that the level of real output remains at y_2 (an under-full employment equilibrium), and cyclical or demand-deficient unemployment persists. Pro-free-market economists disagree. In their view, flexible prices and wage rates, which quickly adjust to market conditions, fall, which in turn means that lower wages and other factor prices reduce firms' costs of production and shift the $SRAS$ curve rightwards to $SRAS_2$. Output moves back to its 'normal capacity' level and the cyclical unemployment has been eliminated.

Real-wage unemployment

Figure 11 illustrates the pre-Keynesian explanation of employment and unemployment, in which full employment is determined as the level of employment where the aggregate demand for labour equals the aggregate supply of labour, at the wage W_{FE}.

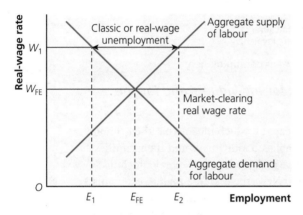

Figure 11 Real-wage unemployment

According to this theory, **real-wage unemployment** is caused by real wage rates being too high, at W_1 rather than W_{FE}. Pre-Keynesians believed that real-wage unemployment is temporary. Market forces would cure the problem by bidding down wages until the number of workers willing to work equals the number that firms wish to hire.

Introducing the concept of the natural rate of unemployment

The **natural rate of unemployment (NRU)** is the rate of unemployment occurring when the aggregate labour market is in equilibrium, i.e. the demand for labour equals the supply of labour. At the natural rate of unemployment, all unemployment is voluntary. In Figure 12 on the next page, the economy's aggregate labour market is in equilibrium at point X, when $AD_L = AS_L$. The market-clearing wage rate is W_{FE} and full employment occurs when E_{FE} workers are hired. However, the curve AS_{LN} shows that E_1 workers are willing and able to work at the full-employment wage rate, but cannot, due to frictional and structural unemployment. If we subtract E_{FE} from E_1 (or X from Z) on the diagram, the natural *level* of unemployment is shown. (The natural *rate* of unemployment is the natural *level* as a percentage of the total labour force.)

Real-wage unemployment is caused when the real wage is too high to clear the aggregate labour market.

Natural rate of unemployment (NRU) The rate of unemployment when the aggregate labour market is in equilibrium.

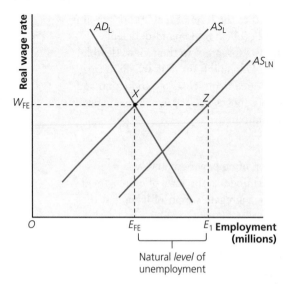

Figure 12 The natural *level* of unemployment

The consequences of unemployment for individuals and for the performance of the economy

Unemployment represents a waste of human capital, which means that the economy is performing inefficiently. Additionally, unemployed individuals and their families suffer from low incomes and spending power, which leads to low morale, feelings of worthlessness and, for some, criminal activity. Nevertheless, free-market economists believe that a certain amount of unemployment is necessary to make the economy function better. By providing downward pressure on wage rates, unemployment may reduce inflationary pressures. However, it tends to widen income differentials and increase absolute and relative poverty. Higher unemployment means greater spending on unemployment and poverty-related benefits, the opportunity cost of which is less spending on the provision of hospitals, schools and other useful resources.

Inflation and deflation

The concepts of inflation, deflation and disinflation

Inflation is defined as a persistent or continuous rise in the price level, or as a fall in the value of money. In the UK there are two main measures of the rate of inflation: the **consumer prices index (CPI)** measure, and the **retail prices index (RPI)** measure. (Page 14 in *Student Guide 2* provides more information on the RPI and the CPI, and also on the two ways in which unemployment is measured in the UK.)

Deflation is the opposite of inflation, being a continuous or persistent fall in the average price level and an accompanying rise in the value of money. Often the word *deflation* is used in a rather looser sense in relation to a contraction of aggregate demand in the economy. Finally, **disinflation** is a slowing down in a positive rate of inflation, without the price level necessarily falling.

> **Exam tip**
> See page 33 to see how you can explain the natural level of unemployment in the context of Phillips curve analysis.

> **Consumer prices index (CPI)** The official measure used to calculate the rate of consumer price inflation in the UK.
>
> **Retail prices index (RPI)** An older measure than the CPI, used to calculate the rate of consumer price inflation in the UK.
>
> **Deflation** Persistent or continuing fall in the average price level.
>
> **Disinflation** When the rate of inflation is falling, but still positive, and the price level is rising more slowly than previously.

> **Exam tip**
> Make sure you don't confuse disinflation with deflation.

Demand-pull and cost-push influences on the price level

Demand-pull inflation is caused by an increase in aggregate demand. Following a rightward shift of the aggregate demand curve, the price level has to rise to persuade firms to produce more output to meet the extra demand. The *AD/AS* diagram in Figure 13 illustrates demand-pull inflation.

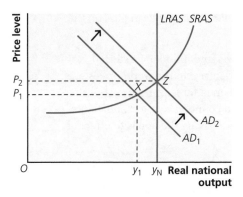

Figure 13 Demand-pull inflation

> **Demand-pull inflation**
> A rising price level caused by an increase in aggregate demand, shown by a shift of the *AD* curve to the right. Also known as demand inflation.

An increase in any of the components of aggregate demand, C, I, G or $(X - M)$, can lead to demand-pull inflation. Increases in consumption spending (C) by households or current government spending (G), for example on public sector pay, may create the extra demand which pulls up the price level.

Figure 13 shows an economy initially producing below the 'normal capacity' level of output, before moving to 'normal capacity' once the *AD* curve has shifted right from AD_1 to AD_2. Initially the equilibrium level of income was determined at point X, but following the shift to AD_2, the economy now produces on its long-run aggregate supply (*LRAS*) curve at 'normal capacity', immediately below point Z. Any further rightward shift of aggregate demand would result in demand-pull inflation, with no permanent increase in real output.

In contrast to demand-pull inflation, **cost-push inflation** can be illustrated by a leftward shift of the short-run *AS* curve. This is shown in Figure 14, where the initial equilibrium level of income was determined at point X. A leftward shift of the *SRAS* curve from $SRAS_1$ to $SRAS_2$, brought about by rising costs of production, means that the equilibrium level of national income and output locates to y_2, which is below point Z.

> **Cost-push inflation**
> A rising price level caused by an increase in costs of production, shown by a shift of the *SRAS* curve to the left. Also known as cost inflation.

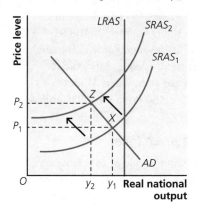

Figure 14 Cost-push inflation

Two variants of cost-push inflation are wage cost-push inflation and import cost-push inflation. Until quite recently, cost-push theory located the cause of inflation in trade union activity and in other causes of market imperfection in both the product (or goods) market and the labour market. In labour markets, their strength enables trade unions to bargain for money wage increases in excess of any rise in labour productivity. Monopoly firms pay these wage increases, partly because of the costs of disrupting production and partly because they believe that they can pass on the increasing costs as price rises.

In recent years, with the decline of trade union power and militancy, external economic shocks, such as that resulting from a sudden rise in the world prices of oil, food and commodities like copper, have been blamed for triggering cost-push inflation. (In 2014 and 2015, however, falling oil and commodity prices, related to a slowdown in China's rate of economic growth, were having the opposite effect of possibly causing deflation.)

Monetarism, the quantity theory of money and the equation of exchange

Around 50 years ago, a group of generally pro-free-market economists became known as **monetarists**. Monetarist economists subscribe to the demand-pull theory of inflation, but they go one stage further by arguing that excess aggregate demand for output is caused solely by a prior increase in the money supply.

The **quantity theory of money** lies at the heart of the monetarist theory of inflation. Suppose the government creates or condones an expansion of the money supply greater than the increase in real national output. As a result, according to the quantity theory, households and firms end up holding excess money balances which, when spent, pull up the price level — provided real output does not expand in line with the increase in spending power.

The starting point for developing the quantity theory is the equation of exchange, devised by an American economist, Irving Fisher, early in the twentieth century:

money supply (stock of money) × the velocity of circulation of money
= price level × quantity of output

or:

$$MV = PQ$$

In the equation, for a particular time period, say a year, the stock of money in the economy (M) multiplied by the velocity of circulation of money (V) equals the price level (P) multiplied by the quantity of real output (Q) in the economy. On the left-hand side of the equation, the velocity of circulation (V) is the speed at which money circulates around the economy when people use money to buy goods. Monetarists have argued that V is constant or at least stable. This means that, when M increases, it is spent on goods and services. If Q is unable to increase, the price level P is pulled up by excess demand.

The effects of expectations on changes in the price level

On page 34, in the context of the **Phillips curve**, we explain the role of expectations of *future* inflation as a cause of *current* inflation. There are two theories of expectations formation it is useful to understand. These are the **theory of adaptive expectations**

Monetarists Economists who believe that inflation is always caused by a prior increase in the money supply or stock of money in the economy.

Quantity theory of money The oldest theory of inflation, incorporated into monetarism, depicted by the equation of exchange: $MV = PQ$.

Phillips curve Shows an apparent relationship between the rate of inflation and the level of unemployment.

Theory of adaptive expectations Argues that expectations of future events should be formed solely on the basis of knowledge of current and recent events.

and the theory of rational expectations. The first of these theories assumes that people form their expectations of the future price level solely by taking into account current and recent changes in the price level. By contrast, the theory of rational expectations argues that it is irrational to take account of a limited set of relevant information (recent and current changes in the price level), when there is a much wider set of relevant information to take into account (such as changes forecast to take place in oil and commodity prices).

Theory of rational expectations Argues that expectations of future events should be formed after taking account of all available relevant knowledge.

The consequences of inflation for both individuals and the performance of the economy

Inflation can impose serious costs both on the economy and on individuals, and the seriousness of these costs depends on whether individuals successfully anticipate the inflation rate. If inflation could be anticipated with complete certainty, some economists argue that it would pose few problems. Households and firms would simply build the expected rate of inflation into their economic decisions, which would not be distorted by wrong guesses.

When inflation is relatively low, with little variation from year to year, it is relatively easy to anticipate next year's inflation rate. Indeed, creeping inflation, which is associated with growing markets, healthy profits and a general climate of business optimism, *greases the wheels* of the economy. Viewed in this way, a low rate of inflation — and not absolute price stability or zero inflation — may be a necessary side-effect or cost of expansionary policies to reduce unemployment.

However, rather than greasing its wheels, inflation may *throw sand in the wheels* of the economy, making it less efficient and competitive. If the 'sand-in the-wheels' effect is stronger than the 'greasing-the-wheels' effect, the costs or disadvantages of inflation exceed the benefits or advantages.

A low but stable inflation rate may also be necessary to make labour markets function efficiently.

The consequences of deflation for both individuals and the performance of the economy

Common sense might suggest that if inflation is generally seen to be bad, its opposite, deflation or a falling price level, must be good, both for the performance of the economy and for individuals. However, extended price deflation may bring its own problems. When people believe prices are going to fall, they may postpone 'big-ticket' consumption decisions, for example replacing their cars. This may erode business confidence and trigger recession or deepen and lengthen an already existing recession. However, this assumes that falling prices are the result of a bad or malign deflation rather than a good or benign deflation.

The difference between the two is illustrated in Figure 15. A good or benign deflation, shown in the left-hand panel of the diagram, results from improvements in the economy's supply side, which reduces business costs of production. Both the *SRAS* curve and the *LRAS* curve shift to the right and, assuming the *AD* curve does not itself shift sufficiently, the price level falls, but output and employment rise. By contrast, a bad or 'malign' deflation, shown in the right-hand panel of the diagram, is caused by a collapse of aggregate demand, and negative multiplier effects.

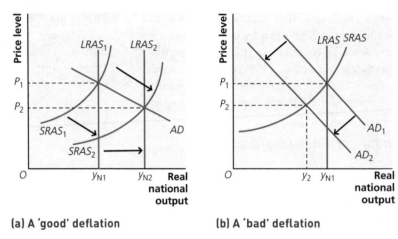

(a) A 'good' deflation   **(b) A 'bad' deflation**

Figure 15 A 'good' and a 'bad' deflation

How changes in world commodity prices affect domestic inflation

In our earlier coverage of the causes of inflation, we mentioned how in some recent years significant increases in the world prices of commodities such as crude oil, industrial raw materials and commodities have led to domestic import-cost-push inflation. It can be argued, however, that at a deeper level such apparent cost-push inflation is in fact caused by excess demand for commodities emanating from emerging market countries such as China. The ultimate engine of domestic inflation lies, therefore, in the conditions which have created global excess demand for commodities.

How changes in other economies can affect inflation in the UK

Following on from the points made in the above paragraph, by changing domestic demand and cost conditions in the UK, economic activity in other economies can affect inflation in the UK. We have already mentioned how first growth, and then the slowing down of growth, in China led respectively to a 'spike' and then a fall in commodity prices. In a different way, economic activity in the USA and the EU has affected UK inflation, primarily because the US and EU markets are so important for British firms. When overseas demand for UK exports is buoyant, British firms can put up their prices.

Possible conflicts between macroeconomic policy objectives

On page 9, we briefly explained the main conflicts between macroeconomic policy objectives facing policy-makers in the UK. In this section of our coverage of economic performance, we discuss further aspects of these conflicts, particularly those related to the Phillips curve.

The short-run Phillips curve and the long-run Phillips curve

Perhaps the best known of all the macroeconomic policy conflicts is the conflict associated with the Phillips curve. The Phillips curve is named after the Keynesian economist A. W. Phillips, who in the 1950s identified an inverse relationship between the rate of inflation and the level of unemployment. The relationship is shown in the Phillips curve diagram in Figure 16.

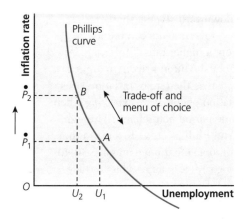

Figure 16 A short-run Phillips curve

The Phillips curve indicates that by using demand management policies, governments can trade off between the number of jobs in the economy and the rate of inflation. Points such as A and B on the short-run Phillips curve represent a menu of choice from which governments can select when deciding an acceptable combination of unemployment and inflation.

The Phillips curve is not a theory of inflation, but it gives support to both the main theories of inflation. In the demand-pull theory, falling unemployment is associated with excess aggregate demand, which pulls up wages and prices. In the cost-push theory, falling unemployment increases the market power of workers in the labour market, enabling them to push for higher wages.

Economists now generally recognise that the Phillips curve in Figure 16 is a **short-run Phillips curve** ($SRPC$), representing the short-run relationship between inflation and unemployment.

In Figure 17, a vertical **long-run Phillips curve** ($LRPC$) has been added to the diagram, cutting the short-run Phillips curve where the rate of inflation is zero. The level of unemployment at this point is the natural level of unemployment, depicted by the symbol U_N, which we explained on page 27. (The long-run Phillips curve is also called the 'L-shaped' Phillips curve.)

Short-run Phillips curve
The original downward-sloping Phillips curve developed by A.W. Phillips.

Long-run Phillips curve
A vertical Phillips curve, developed by Milton Friedman and Edmund Phelps, along which trade-offs between reducing inflation and reducing unemployment are not possible. Also called the 'L-shaped' Phillips curve.

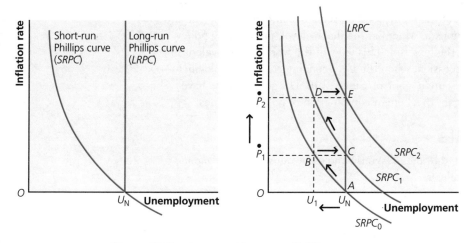

Figure 17 Short-run and long-run Phillips curves

If you look back to Figure 16, you will see that the downward-sloping short-run Phillips curve appears to offer a menu of choice. Governments can reduce unemployment, but only if they are prepared to accept a higher rate of inflation. However, in the 1960s, the leading monetarist economist Milton Friedman argued that in the long run this could not be achieved. As soon as the rate of inflation rises above zero, *current* inflation is above the rate of inflation people were *expecting* when they formed their expectations of inflation in the time period beforehand. Through a rather complicated process, this causes the short-run Phillips curve to shift to the right. (Friedman used the theory of adaptive expectations, mentioned on page 30, to explain the process.) The end result is that in the long run, it is impossible to trade off between reducing unemployment and controlling inflation. Policy-makers are faced with a vertical long-run Phillips curve, located at the natural level (or rate) of unemployment, along which trade-offs are not possible.

[handwritten margin note: TRADE OFF]

The implications of the short-run and long-run Phillips curves for economic policy

As mentioned, the downward-sloping short-run Phillips curve offers policy-makers a menu of choice between reducing unemployment and controlling inflation. However, the vertical long-run Phillips curve (or 'L-shaped' Phillips curve) offers no such choice. There can be no trade-off between inflation and unemployment in the long run.

Monetarist and other free-market economists argue that, in the long run, the only way to keep unemployment below the NRU is to permit the money supply to increase so as to finance an ever-accelerating inflation. But an accelerating inflation will eventually accelerate out of control, which, in the resulting breakdown of economic activity, will almost certainly shift the long-run Phillips curve to the right and increase the NRU. Any attempt to reduce unemployment below the NRU is therefore foolhardy and irresponsible. In the short run it accelerates inflation, while in the long run it perversely increases the NRU to an unnecessarily high level.

Reconciling policy conflicts in the short run and the long run

We have mentioned that governments have sometimes attempted to reconcile policy conflicts by trading off between apparently mutually exclusive policy objectives. Many supply-side economists argue, however, that provided pro-free-market supply-side policies are implemented, at the micro-level markets become more efficient and competitive, producing conditions in which, at the macro-level, pre-existing policy conflicts can be reconciled in the long run. This view of the world was prevalent in the decade before the 2008 recession, when the UK economy grew, unemployment fell, and inflation was generally under control. Since 2010, UK governments have been trying to achieve once again this benign combination of policy outcomes.

Examination skills

The skills most likely to be tested by data-response and essay questions on *economic performance* at A-level are as follows:

- Understanding economic growth and its relation to the economic cycle
- Knowledge of the main types of unemployment
- Analysis of demand-pull and cost-push inflation
- Drawing and interpretation of Phillips curve diagrams

Examination questions

Examination questions on *economic performance* are likely to cover economic growth, the economic cycle, the causes of and interrelationships between unemployment and inflation, deflation and the Phillips curve. EQ1 in the Questions & Answers section of this guide is on unemployment, while MCQs 7, 8 and 9 are respectively on economic growth, the economic cycle, and on the natural rate of unemployment, inflation and the Phillips curve.

Common examination errors

Commonly made mistakes on *economic performance* include:

- inaccurate drawing of diagrams to show economic growth, the economic cycle, cyclical unemployment, demand-pull and cost-push inflation and the Phillips curve
- confusing frictional and structural unemployment
- confusing inflation with a one-off price change, or with relative price changes
- failing to appreciate conflicts between achieving the macroeconomic policy objectives of full employment and price stability
- assuming that inflation is always bad and never good, and that therefore deflation must be good because inflation is bad
- confusing short-run and long-run Phillips curves and also confusing these with with *AD/AS* diagrams
- confusing a reduction of unemployment below the NRU with a shift to the left of the NRU

Summary

- Economic growth divides into short-run and long-run economic growth.
- Total unemployment is measured by the Labour Force Survey method and by the claimant count.
- Types of unemployment include frictional, structural and cyclical (demand-deficient) unemployment, together with real-wage unemployment.
- Different types of unemployment require different policy solutions.
- Unemployment is bad because it involves a waste of resources.
- The rate of inflation, which is defined as a persistent increase in the average price level, is measured by the consumer prices index and by the retail prices index.

- Inflation is caused by both demand-pull and cost-push factors.
- It is important to distinguish between the causes and the effects of both unemployment and inflation.
- The costs of inflation are generally assumed to exceed the benefits of inflation.
- The short-run Phillips curve, named after the Keynesian economist A.W. Phillips, is a statistical relationship showing an inverse or negative relationship between the rate of price inflation and the level of unemployment.
- The Phillips curve is not itself a theory of inflation.

■ 4.2.4 Financial markets and monetary policy

These notes relate to AQA specification section 4.2.4 and prepare you to answer examination questions on:

- the structure of financial markets and financial assets
- commercial banks and investment banks
- central banks and monetary policy
- the regulation of the financial system

Essential information
The structure of financial markets and financial assets
The characteristics and functions of money

Money is best defined by focusing on the two principal functions it performs in the economy. Money functions as:

- a medium of exchange or means of payment
- a store of value or store of wealth

Money has two other functions, which are less important for you to know. It serves as a measure of value and as a standard of deferred payment; and it is the unit in which the prices of goods are quoted and in which accounts are kept.

Knowledge check 7
What is meant by a standard of deferred payment?

Definitions of the money supply and the distinction between narrow money and broad money

Over the years, the Bank of England has used more than one definition of the money supply. These divide into measures of narrow money and broad money.

- Narrow money, which restricts the measure of money to cash and bank and building society sight deposits (current account deposits), reflects the medium-of-exchange function of money, namely money functioning as a means of payment.
- Broad money also includes other financial assets which, although stores of value, are too illiquid, at least for the time being, to function as mediums of exchange.

The difference between the money market, the capital market and the foreign exchange market

A financial market is a market in financial assets or securities. Financial markets can be classified in a number of ways, but one of the most fruitful is as markets for short-dated financial assets (often called money markets) and markets for long-dated and undated financial assets (often called capital markets). There are also foreign exchange markets, and markets for commodity futures and insurance products.

Exam tip
Make sure you understand the similarities of, and the differences between, money markets and capital markets.

Money Primarily a medium of exchange, but also a store of value.

Medium of exchange Means of payment.

Store of value Means of holding wealth.

Narrow money The part of the stock of money (or money supply) made up of cash and liquid bank and building society deposits.

Broad money The part of the stock of money (or money supply) made up of cash, other liquid assets such as bank and building society deposits, but also some less liquid assets.

Financial market A market in financial assets or securities.

Money markets Provide a means for lenders and borrowers to satisfy their short-term financial needs.

Capital markets Provide a means for lenders and borrowers to satisfy their long-term financial needs.

Foreign exchange markets (forex, FX, or currency markets) Global, decentralised markets for the trading of currencies.

The role of financial markets in the wider economy

Without the existence of financial markets, which of course include banking markets, modern economies would not be able to function. If financial markets did not exist, the supply of liquidity necessary to finance economic transactions would dry up. The fundamental purpose of financial markets is to act as intermediaries which channel funds from those who have surplus funds to those who have a shortage of funds. And without foreign exchange markets, it would become very difficult, if not impossible, for international trade and tourism to take place.

The difference between debt and equity

Debt is what people *owe*, equity is what they *own*. To explain this, consider a company which needs to raise money to finance its expansion. If it borrows, the company is increasing its debt. To avoid accumulating debt, the company may decide to sell new shares, in which case it is selling ownership in itself. The new shareholders, who have become part-owners of the company, have increased their equity stakes in the company.

Why there is an inverse relationship between market interest rates and bond prices?

When companies borrow, they may sell a form of company debt known as corporate bonds. Likewise, government bonds are a form of government debt. In the UK these are called gilt-edge securities, or gilts.

Consider a £100.00 government bond which pays the bond holder a guaranteed £5.00 a year in interest. If the bond price remains at £100.00, the bond holder earns a 5% annual interest payment. Suppose, however, that the long-term interest rate increases to 10%. In this situation, the second-hand price of the £100.00 bond must fall on the stock exchange to £50.00 to convert the £5.00 guaranteed annual interest payment into a yield of 10%. There is thus an inverse or negative relationship between the bond's price and the rate of interest the bond earns if it is sold second-hand on the stock exchange.

Commercial banks and investment banks

The difference between a commercial bank and an investment bank

Commercial banks, which are often called retail banks and 'high street' banks, are commercially run financial institutions that deal with ordinary members of the general public and businesses.

Although they are also profit-making and commercially run institutions, investment banks such as the US-owned Goldman Sachs, are mainly involved in helping companies, other financial institutions and other organisations (such as the government and its agencies) to raise finance by selling shares or bonds to investors and to hedge against risks.

The main functions of a commercial bank

The main function of a commercial bank, acting as an intermediary between households and firms, is to accept deposits from the general public that can be transferred by cheque, by debit card or through an online transfer of funds undertaken on the internet, and to create deposits which are lent to customers who

Liquidity Measures the ease with which an asset can be converted into cash without loss of value. Cash is the most liquid of all assets.

Debt What people owe.

Equity What people own.

Commercial banks Financial institutions which make profits by selling banking services to their customers. Also known as retail banks and 'high street' banks.

Investment banks Financial institutions which do not generally accept deposits from ordinary members of the general public. Investment banks provide financial advice to private-sector companies and to the government.

wish to borrow from their banks. Commercial banks do have other functions, such as buying and selling foreign exchange, but these are less important.

The structure of a commercial bank's balance sheet and its need to maintain liquidity, profitability and security

Prudent retail banking requires a commercial bank to operate on a ratio of cash and other liquid assets to advances that maintains customers' confidence in the bank, while generating acceptable profits for the bank. In other words, prudent banking involves trading off liquidity against profitability.

Besides trading off between liquidity and profitability, banks also have to make choices with regard to the security of their assets. The profitability for banks of loans granted to customers depends to a significant extent on the degree of risk attached to the loans. Non-secured loans are risky because if a customer defaults on the loan, the bank cannot recover any money. Because of the risk of non-repayment of unsecured loans, banks charge higher interest rates, and hence make more profit than is the case with secured loans such as mortgage loans.

Potential conflicts between these objectives

The asset structure shown in Table 1 illustrates the conflict between liquidity and profitability facing a commercial bank.

Table 1 The asset structure of a commercial bank

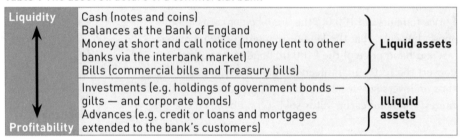

If a bank kept all its assets in the most liquid form of cash, it would not really be a bank at all, but a safe-deposit institution. The bank's profits would come largely from the fees it charged customers for guarding their valuables. The bank's cash would be completely liquid, but not at all profitable.

The cash a bank holds allows it to make profitable advances or loans to its customers. The rates of interest that retail banks charge on the loans are a major source of profits. Imprudent or greedy banks might be tempted to create far too many profitable advances — imprudent in the sense that the banks possess insufficient cash to meet customers' possible cash withdrawals. These banks would be operating on too low a ratio of cash and other liquid assets to the advances they have created. If a run on the banks occurred, the banks would crash.

A conflict stemming from a lack of security of bank assets is illustrated by events which happened in the American financial crisis in 2007 and 2008. American banks sought profit through providing sub-prime mortgage loans to high-risk customers.

> **Knowledge check 8**
>
> Why is cash, which is the most liquid of all assets, not profitable?

These loans turned into bad debts when customers could not repay the loans. Saddled with bad debts, a number of banks went out of business, the most notable being Lehmann Brothers in the USA in 2008.

How banks create credit and bank deposits

In a modern monetary economy, bank deposits which are created by commercial banks form by far the largest part of the money supply or stock of money in an economy. Cash acts as the 'small change' of the total money stock. To illustrate the credit- and bank-deposit-creating process, we shall assume that there is only one commercial bank in the economy, possessing only one reserve asset (cash) and that to maintain confidence, the bank must always possess cash equal to 10% of total customer deposits.

A member of the general public deposits £1,000 cash in the bank. From the bank's point of view, both its assets and its liabilities increase by £1,000. The cash is the bank's asset, but the £1,000 deposit credited in the customer's name is the bank's liability, since the bank is liable to honour any cash withdrawals made by the customer. The £1,000 is recorded in the bank's balance sheet in the following way:

Assets	Liabilities
£1,000	£1,000
Total assets: £1,000	**Total liabilities: £1,000**

As things stand, all the bank's deposit liabilities are backed with cash (that is, the bank's cash ratio is 100%). But at the next stage, the bank uses the cash as a monetary base from which to launch the profitable loans it grants to customers. Unlike the customer depositing the £1,000, other customers may need to borrow from the bank. The 10% cash ratio the bank has chosen to work with means that the bank is in a position to lend exactly £9,000 to these customers. This takes the form of an interest-earning advance on the assets side of the bank's balance sheet, which is matched by a £9,000 created deposit on the liabilities side:

Assets	Liabilities
£1,000	£1,000
Advances: £9,000	Created deposits: £9,000
Total assets: £10,000	**Total liabilities: £10,000**

Both the customer who made the initial deposit of £1,000 and the customers in receipt of the advances can draw cheques or make payments equal to £10,000 in total on their deposits. The initial £1,000 cash deposit has enabled total deposits to be increased to £10,000. The bank has created new credit and bank deposits to the tune of £9,000.

Central banks and monetary policy

The main functions of a central bank

A **central bank** such as the Bank of England has two key functions: to help the government maintain macroeconomic stability and to bring about financial stability in the monetary system. With regard to macroeconomic stability, the Bank of England's remit is to deliver price stability and, subject to that, to support the government's economic objectives, including those for growth and employment.

Financial stability can be achieved, in part, through the central bank acting as lender of last resort to the banking system, and also, in part, by the central bank's monitoring

Exam tip

It is important to understand that most of the money supply or stock of money in the economy is deposit money rather than cash.

....

Central bank A national bank that provides financial and banking services for its country's government and banking system, as well as implementing the government's monetary policy and issuing currency. The Bank of England is the UK's central bank.

and regulation of the financial system. The lender-of-last-resort function can be defined as the readiness of the central bank to extend loans to banks that are solvent but have short-term liquidity problems.

Central banks also carry out other related functions such as: controlling the note issue, acting as the bankers' bank, acting as the government's bank, buying and selling currencies to influence the exchange rate, and liaising with overseas central banks and international organisations.

Monetary policy and its objectives

The main function of the Bank of England is to implement monetary policy on behalf of the UK government.

For over 30 years, control of inflation has been the main objective of UK monetary policy. The government, in the person of the chancellor of the exchequer, sets the inflation rate target, which since 2003 has been 2% CPI inflation, and instructs the Bank of England to operate monetary policy so as to 'hit' this target.

However, in the 2008/09 recession, negative economic growth and growing unemployment led to a situation in which controlling inflation as the main monetary policy objective was temporarily placed on the back burner, with monetary policy being used instead to try and increase aggregate demand and bring about recovery. Although the Bank's primary objective is price stability, it must also support the government's economic policy objectives, including those for growth and employment.

The role of the Bank of England's Monetary Policy Committee

The Treasury abandoned its hands-on role in implementing monetary policy in 1997, when the government made the Bank of England operationally independent. The Bank of England now sets Bank Rate independently of the government.

At the same time as the Bank of England was made operationally independent, within the Bank, the Monetary Policy Committee (MPC) was created. If the Bank wishes to pursue an expansionary monetary policy to boost spending in the economy, usually when the CPI inflation rate is *below* 2%, the MPC will cut Bank Rate. Conversely, if the Bank wishes to pursue a contractionary monetary, usually when the CPI inflation rate is *above* 2%, the MPC will increase Bank Rate.

The factors considered by the MPC when setting Bank Rate

Indicators that are of interest to the MPC before any Bank Rate decision include:

- the unemployment rate
- the level of saving
- changes in retail sales
- adverse external shocks, such as a Middle East war
- the state of consumer and/or business confidence
- the state of the housing market and the market for mortgages
- movements in the pound's exchange rate

The effect of changes in the exchange rate

The effects of changes in the exchange rate on the economy can be quite complicated. We shall describe only one line of reasoning. In the first place, a fall in the exchange

---

Knowledge check 9

What is the difference between monetary policy and fiscal policy?

Monetary policy Implemented by the government and the central bank (in the UK, the Bank of England) to achieve policy objectives (e.g. control of inflation) using monetary instruments (e.g. Bank Rate and quantitative easing).

Bank Rate The interest rate set by the Bank of England which the Bank uses as a benchmark for setting the interest rates that it charges when lending to commercial banks and other financial institutions.

Monetary Policy Committee (MPC) Implements UK monetary policy on behalf of the Bank of England, primarily by setting Bank Rate.

rate makes exports more price competitive in world markets and imports less price competitive in the UK market. As a result, the UK's balance of payments on current account improves. And since net export demand is a component of aggregate demand, the economy's *AD* curve shifts to the right.

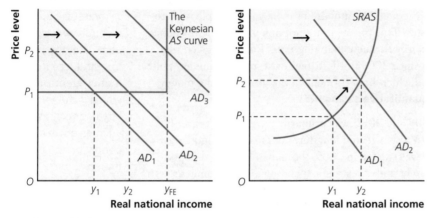

Figure 18 The effect of a fall in the exchange rate on aggregate demand

What happens next depends on whether there was significant unemployment in the economy *before* the exchange rate fell, and on the slope of the *SRAS* curve to the right of the initial point of macroeconomic equilibrium. Figure 18 depicts a situation in which growth of real output and inflation occur after the rightward shift of the *AD* curve. If the increase in the price level is deemed by the MPC to be too high, the Committee might decide to raise Bank Rate in order to take demand out of the economy.

The monetary policy transmission mechanism

The Bank of England believes that interest rate policy affects aggregate demand and inflation through a number of channels, which form the transmission mechanism of monetary policy. The flow chart in Figure 19 shows the routes through which changes in Bank Rate (the instrument of monetary policy), shown at point 1 in the diagram, eventually affect inflation (the objective of monetary policy), shown at point 11. (To research more detail of how the transmission mechanism operates, read Case Study 8.3 on pages 250 and 251 of *AQA A-level Economics 2* published by Hodder Education, 2016.)

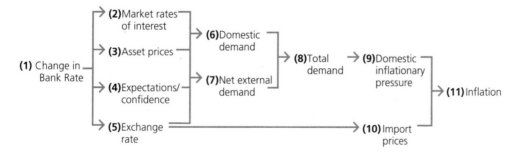

Figure 19 The transmission mechanism of interest rate policy

How the Bank of England can influence the growth of the money supply

For many decades, the Bank of England has been operating an *accommodating* monetary policy, in which it allows the money supply to increase or decrease so that the stock of money in the economy equals the amount of money that people wish to hold at current market interest rates. This means that the Bank of England influences the growth of money supply, primarily through changing Bank Rate. But given that Bank Rate has been held at 0.5% since 2009 until 2016 at least, other monetary policy instruments have been introduced which have influenced the growth of the money supply. The main one has been **quantitative easing (QE)**.

QE, which was used between 2009 and 2012, was primarily meant to increase the money supply directly — though it also affected long-term interest rates and hence the demand for loans. When QE was started in 2009, the Bank of England hoped that it would help to revive consumer and investment spending and economic growth. People often think that QE involves increasing the money supply by printing new banknotes. However, QE was not as simple as this. The Bank of England described QE's transmission route in the following way:

> Direct injections of money into the economy, primarily by buying gilts, can have a number of effects. The sellers of the assets have more money so may go out and spend it. That will help to boost growth. Or they may buy other assets instead, such as shares or company bonds. That will push up the prices of those assets, making the people who own them, either directly or through their pension funds, better off. So they may go out and spend more. And higher asset prices mean lower yields, which brings down the cost of borrowing for businesses and households. That should provide a further boost to spending. In addition, banks will find themselves holding more reserves. That might lead them to boost their lending to consumers and businesses. So, once again, borrowing increases and so does spending.

The regulation of the financial system

Regulation of the financial system in the UK

Financial regulation involves limiting the freedom of banks and other financial institutions, and of the people they employ, to behave as they otherwise might wish to do. Financial regulation is undertaken by the Financial Policy Committee (FPC) at the Bank of England, by the Prudential Regulation Authority (PRA) — itself a part of the Bank of England — and by the Financial Conduct Authority (FCA), which is not part of the Bank. Through the FPC, the Bank of England has responsibility for the Bank's second key function: maintaining financial stability.

The FPC is primarily responsible for macroprudential regulation, whereas the PRA and FCA are mainly responsible for microprudential regulation.

- Macroprudential regulation is concerned with identifying, monitoring and acting to remove risks that affect the stability of the financial system as a whole.
- Microprudential regulation focuses on ensuring the stability of individual banks and other financial institutions. It involves identifying, monitoring and managing risks that relate to individual firms.

Quantitative easing (QE)
An unconventional form of monetary policy through which a central bank, e.g. the Bank of England, creates new money electronically which it then uses to buy financial assets, such as government bonds, on the country's financial markets. Also known as the Asset Purchase Scheme.

Exam tip

Regulation of the financial system is a new part of the AQA A-level specification and may not be covered in old textbooks.

Bank failures

Bank failures occur because banks are financial institutions which 'borrow short but lend long'. Much of the assets that commercial banks possess results from the creation of deposit liabilities which customers can instantly withdraw. However, the banks' assets are largely long term, often in the form of 25-year mortgages granted to finance house purchase. Banks can also fall victim to rogue bank workers who steal huge amounts of money from the banks that employ them.

Liquidity ratios and capital ratios

Over time, banks have failed or required government assistance either because they lacked liquidity, or because they had inadequate capital, or through a combination of both of these contributory factors.

A bank's **liquidity ratio** is the ratio of cash and other liquid assets owned by the bank to its deposit liabilities. Liquidity is a measure of the ability and ease with which assets can be converted to cash. To remain viable, a bank must have enough liquid assets to meet its near-term obligations, such as withdrawals of cash by depositors.

A bank's **capital ratio** is the amount of capital on a bank's balance sheet as a proportion of its loans. If banks do not have sufficient capital, they are at risk if the value of their assets falls.

While insufficient liquidity makes a bank vulnerable to a run on the bank, insufficient capital exposes the bank to the risk of a fall in the value of its assets.

Moral hazard

As the 2007/08 financial crisis showed, banks are sometimes tempted to take too many risks in pursuing the huge profits that lending long allows. They do this because they believe that the Bank of England, in its role as lender of last resort, and the government through its bailouts, will not allow banks to fail.

Moral hazard exists when a bank pursues profit and takes on too much risk in the knowledge that, if things go wrong, someone else will bear a significant portion of the cost. Investing in high-risk assets can lead to high profits, but unless there is the possibility that financial institutions will be allowed to fail, there is insufficient incentive for them to act prudently.

Systemic risk and the impact of problems that arise in financial markets upon the real economy

It is important to distinguish between systemic and one-off risks. In contrast to a one-off shock which affects only a single bank without rippling into the rest of the banking system, **systemic risk** affects the entire banking system and other financial institutions as well. The consequences of a systemic financial crisis can be devastating because of the role that banks and finance play in the wider economy.

Examination skills

The skills most likely to be tested by data-response and essay questions on *financial markets and monetary policy* at A-level are as follows:

- Displaying relevant knowledge of how UK financial markets operate
- Understanding the functions of commercial banks and investment banks

Liquidity ratio The ratio of a bank's cash and other liquid assets to its deposits.

Capital ratio The amount of capital on a bank's balance sheet as a proportion of its loans.

Moral hazard The tendency of individuals and firms, once protected against some contingency, to behave so as to make that contingency more likely.

Systemic risk In a financial context, this refers to the risk of a breakdown of the entire financial system, caused by inter-linkages within the system, rather than simply the failure of an individual bank or financial institution within the system.

- Appreciating how commercial banks create credit and new bank deposits
- Relating monetary policy to the control of inflation
- Understanding the links between, and also the differences between, monetary policy and fiscal policy

Examination questions

Examination questions on *financial markets and monetary policy* are likely to focus mainly on monetary policy, though questions may also be set on how financial markets function and on how commercial banks create bank deposits and credit. In the Questions & Answers section of this guide, EQ 2 is set on monetary policy, while MCQs 10 and 11 are respectively on financial markets and monetary policy.

Common examination errors

Commonly made mistakes on *financial markets and monetary policy* include:
- failing to appreciate what financial markets do
- confusing monetary policy instruments such as Bank Rate with the policy objective of controlling inflation
- failing to realise that bank deposits are the main form of modern money
- not understanding that Bank Rate policy becomes ineffective as inflation approaches zero
- not appreciating the links between monetary policy and the exchange rate
- failure to understand how quantitative easing works

Summary

- Money markets, capital markets and foreign exchange markets are the main financial markets.
- Money is defined by its medium-of-exchange and store-of-value functions.
- The commercial banking system creates bank deposits and credit which are a multiple of the cash deposited in the system.
- Monetary policy is the part of macroeconomic policy which uses policy instruments such as Bank Rate and quantitative easing to achieve objectives such as the control of inflation.
- As bank deposits are the main form of money, to be successful, monetary policy must aim to control the rate of growth of bank deposits.
- Bank Rate has generally been the most important monetary policy instrument, though recently quantitative easing has temporarily been used.
- Since the 1990s, the rate of inflation has been the main monetary policy objective, but since the 2008/09 recession, achieving 2% inflation has been subordinated to stimulating aggregate demand to promote economic recovery.

■ 4.2.5 Fiscal policy and supply-side policies

These notes relate to AQA specification section 4.2.5 and prepare you to answer examination questions on:

■ fiscal policy

■ supply-side policies

Essential information

Fiscal policy

What fiscal policy involves

Fiscal policy involves the manipulation of government spending, taxation and the budget balance by the government (the Treasury) to try to achieve whatever policy objectives the government has in mind. Using the symbols G for government spending and T for taxation and other sources of revenue, the three possible budgetary positions a government can have are:

$G = T$: balanced budget

$G > T$: budget deficit

$G < T$: budget surplus

Fiscal policy can have both macroeconomic and microeconomic functions

For many years, fiscal policy was generally associated with the demand-side macroeconomic management of the level of aggregate demand. However, supply-side fiscal policy, which has important microeconomic dimensions, has become important in recent decades.

Other microeconomic aspects of fiscal policy are explained in *Student Guide 3* in the context of government intervention to correct microeconomic market failures.

How fiscal policy can be used to influence aggregate demand

Demand-side fiscal policy or Keynesian fiscal policy operates through increasing or decreasing aggregate demand. Government spending (G) is one of the components of aggregate demand. An increase in government spending or a cut in taxation increases the size of the budget deficit (or reduces the size of the budget surplus). Either way, an injection into the circular flow of income occurs and the effect on aggregate demand is expansionary. Conversely, a cut in government spending or an increase in taxation reduces the size of the budget deficit (or increases the size of the budget surplus). A withdrawal of spending from the circular flow of income occurs and the effect on aggregate demand is contractionary.

> **Knowledge check 10**
>
> What is the difference between a budget deficit and a budget surplus?

How fiscal policy can be used to influence aggregate supply

Supply-side fiscal policy, which is favoured by free-market-oriented supply-side economists, focuses on shifting the long-run aggregate supply (*LRAS*) curve, rather than the *AD* curve, to the right. This is shown in Figure 20.

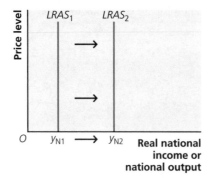

Figure 20 A rightward-shift of the *LRAS* curve brought about by supply-side fiscal policy

Supply-side policy fiscal policy tries to alter at the microeconomic level the incentives facing economic agents. Income tax cuts may make people work harder, while cuts in the real value of unemployment benefits (compared to disposable income in work) may encourage unskilled and low-paid workers to choose work rather than unemployment. Supply-side tax cuts may also encourage saving, investment and an entrepreneurial culture.

How government spending and taxation can affect the pattern of economic activity

At the macro level, fiscal policy largely affects the *level* of economic activity. By contrast, at the micro level, fiscal policy affects the *pattern* of economic activity, for example by increasing provision of public goods and merit goods. Expenditure taxes and subsidies are also used to alter the relative prices of goods and services so as to encourage people to switch their spending away from, say, sugary drinks and into healthier forms of nutrition.

The types of and reasons for public expenditure

Current public spending is short term and has to be renewed each year, whereas government capital spending is long-term spending on 'social capital' and does not have to be renewed each year.

Public spending can also be divided into *programme spending,* which is decided on by programme departments such as the Department of Health, subject to overall Treasury control, and *demand-led spending,* for example on unemployment benefits and the state pension. Spending on unemployment benefits is literally led by demand, increasing when unemployment grows and falling when unemployment drops. Demand-led spending changes according to the phases of the economic cycle and, in the case of demand-led spending on the state pension, according to how long elderly people live.

There are numerous reasons for public spending. These include:

- supplying goods and services that the private sector would fail to provide
- to achieve supply-side improvements, for example spending on training to improve labour productivity
- to spend on pollution controls to reduce the negative effects of externalities
- to subsidise industries needing financial support
- to help redistribute income to achieve more equity

Why governments levy taxes

The main reason for taxation is to raise the revenue required to finance government spending. It follows that the reasons why governments levy taxes are basically the same as the reasons we have explained in the previous section for public expenditure. Governments use taxation, along with government spending, in the macro and micro management of the economy. In terms of *resource allocation*, taxes are used to alter relative prices and patterns of consumption. In terms of *distribution*, if the government decides that the distributions of income and wealth produced by free-market forces are undesirable, taxation and transfers in its public spending programme can be used to modify these distributions and reduce the alleged market failure resulting from inequity.

The difference between direct and indirect taxes

Income tax is an example of a **direct tax** because the person who receives and benefits from the income is liable in law to have to pay the tax to the government; they cannot pass the tax on to someone else. By contrast, a tax on spending, such as value added tax (VAT) or an excise duty such as the duty on tobacco, is an **indirect tax**. This is because the seller of the good, and not the buyer who benefits from its consumption, is liable to pay the tax. However, the buyer indirectly pays some of the tax, via a price rise.

The difference between progressive, proportional and regressive taxes

A tax is progressive when the proportion of income paid in tax rises as income increases. **Progressive taxation**, combined with transfers to lower-income groups, reduces the spending power of the rich, while increasing that of the poor.

Some taxes, particularly those designed to reduce consumption of the demerit goods alcohol and tobacco, fall more heavily on the poor. These taxes are regressive. **Regressive taxation** means that the proportion of income paid in tax falls as income increases.

In recent years, many economists and politicians, usually of a pro-free-market persuasion, have advocated the introduction of proportional taxation. In the case of a proportional income tax, this is sometimes called a 'flat tax'.

The principles of taxation

In order to assess whether a tax is good or bad, a starting point is to judge it against the principles of taxation.

- *Economy* means a tax should be cheap to collect in relation to the revenue it yields.
- *Convenience* and *certainty* mean that a tax should be convenient for taxpayers to pay and that taxpayers should be reasonably sure of the amount of tax they will be required to pay to the government.

Direct tax A tax which cannot be shifted by the person legally liable to pay the tax onto someone else. Direct taxes are levied on income and wealth.

Indirect tax A tax which can be shifted by the person legally liable to pay the tax onto someone else, for example through raising the price of a good being sold by the taxpayer.

Progressive tax A tax is progressive if, as income rises, a greater proportion of income is paid to the government in tax.

Regressive tax A tax is regressive if, as income rises, a smaller proportion of income is paid to the government in tax.

Knowledge check 11

Is a direct tax the same as a progressive tax?

- *Equity* means a tax system should be fair.
- *Efficiency* requires a tax to achieve its desired objective(s) with minimum undesired side-effects or unintended consequences.
- Finally, to comply with the principle of *flexibility*, a tax must be easy to change to meet new circumstances.

A 'good' tax meets as many of these principles as possible, although because of conflicts and trade-offs, it is usually impossible for a tax to meet them all at the same time.

The role and relative merits of different UK taxes
Some of the main taxes levied in the UK are as follows:
- Income tax. This is the UK's main direct tax. It is paid on earnings, pensions, benefits, savings and investment income, and rents. As a progressive tax, income tax reduces post-tax income inequalities, but this merit is reduced by the fact that national insurance contributions (NICs), which in effect are a second income tax, are quite regressive.
- Corporation tax. This is a tax on company profits.
- Value added tax (VAT) and excise duties. These are expenditure taxes. They have the advantage of allowing the government to influence the pattern of spending in the UK, but on the other hand they are generally regressive.

The relationship between the budget balance and the national debt
The relationship between the budget balance and the national debt provides an example of the difference between a *flow* and a *stock*. A budget deficit occurs whenever the flow of government spending exceeds the flow of tax and other sources of revenue. The resulting flow of government borrowing which finances a budget deficit adds to the stock of the national debt. Conversely, when there is a budget surplus, the government's surplus tax revenue can be used to pay back a fraction of past government borrowing. This reduces the size of the national debt.

Cyclical and structural budget deficits and surpluses
The cyclical budget deficit is the part of an overall budget deficit that rises and falls with the upswings and downswings of the economic cycle. The cyclical deficit falls in the recovery and boom phases of the economic cycle — perhaps moving into surplus in the boom — but it increases when growth slows down and the economy is threatened with recession. In the upswing of the economic cycle, tax revenues rise and spending on welfare benefits falls. By contrast, in the downswing, tax revenues fall but public spending on unemployment and poverty-related welfare benefits increases. As a result, the government's finances deteriorate.

The structural budget deficit is the portion of a country's budget deficit that is unrelated to changes in the economic cycle. The structural deficit will exist even when the economy is at the peak of the cycle. The structural deficit results from fundamental imbalance in government tax revenues and public spending, and is not caused by short-term fluctuations in tax revenues and expenditures.

Budget balance The balance between government spending and government revenue.

National debt Accumulated stock of past central government borrowing that has not as yet been paid back.

Cyclical budget deficit The part of the budget deficit which rises in the downswing of the economic cycle and falls in the upswing of the cycle.

Structural budget deficit The part of the budget deficit which is not affected by the economic cycle but results from structural factors in the economy which affect the government's finances.

> **Exam tip**
> Make sure you don't confuse the cyclical deficit with the similar-sounding cyclically adjusted deficit.

The consequences of budget deficits and surpluses for macroeconomic performance

Keynesian economists argue that governments should use budget deficits and surpluses to actively manage the level of aggregate demand. By so doing, purposeful or 'smart' government intervention can promote economic growth and smooth the economic cycle. Anti-Keynesian economists disagree, arguing that discretionary fiscal policy destabilises the economy, slows the growth process and leads to 'crowding out', which occurs when an increase in public spending causes private sector spending to fall.

However, Keynesians and anti-Keynesians agree that **automatic stabilisers** should be used to smooth or dampen cyclical fluctuations in the economy. Suppose, for example, that an adverse demand shock causes aggregate demand and national income to fall. As national income falls and unemployment rises, demand-led public spending on unemployment pay and welfare benefits also rises, but tax revenues fall. This injects demand back into the economy, thereby stabilising and dampening the deflationary impact of the initial fall in aggregate demand, and reducing the overall size of the contractionary multiplier effect. Automatic stabilisers also operate in the opposite direction to dampen the expansionary effect of an increase in aggregate demand.

The significance of the size of the national debt

To understand the significance, if any, of the size of the national debt, we must distinguish between the **nominal national debt** and the **real national debt**. The nominal national debt is the national debt measured at its cash value in the year in question. Whenever there is a budget deficit, the nominal national debt grows in size. However, Keynesian economists argue that it is the *real* national debt and not the *nominal* national debt that is important. The real national debt is the nominal national debt as a ratio of nominal GDP. If the nominal debt is increasing by, say, 4% a year but the nominal GDP is increasing by 6% a year, the real national debt actually falls. When this happens, growth of the nominal national debt does not necessarily pose problems for the economy.

The role of the Office for Budget Responsibility

The **Office for Budget Responsibility (OBR)** provides independent analysis of the UK's public sector finances by twice a year publishing medium-term forecasts of the UK economy. And instead of the chancellor making judgements based on Treasury forecasts, the OBR rules on whether the government's policy has a better than 50% chance of meeting the Treasury's fiscal targets.

Supply-side policies

The difference between supply-side policies and supply-side improvements in the economy

Supply-side *policies* are the set of government policies, micro as well as macro, which aim to improve national economic performance by creating competitive and more efficient markets. By contrast, supply-side *reform* or supply-side improvements take place within the economy's private sector without being brought about explicitly by government policy. Nevertheless, a major aim of supply-side policies is to encourage the reform of markets and the ways in which the economy's supply side operates.

Automatic stabilisers Factors within tax and public spending systems that automatically tend to dampen the economic cycle.

Nominal national debt The cash value at a particular point in time of accumulated government borrowing.

Real national debt The nominal national debt as a ratio of nominal national income or GDP.

Office for Budget Responsibility (OBR) Advisory public body that provides independent economic forecasts and analysis of the public finances as background to the preparation of the UK budget.

> **Exam tip**
>
> Make sure you can appreciate the differences between, and also the similarities of, the Bank of England's Monetary Policy Committee and the Office for Budget Responsibility.

How supply-side policies can help to achieve supply-side improvements in the economy

Two of the ways in which supply-side policies try to create competitive and more efficient markets are by:

- increasing personal incentives, by, for example, cutting rates of personal income tax, so as to make it worthwhile for individuals to work harder, to save, to invest and to undertake risky entrepreneurial activities
- deregulating the economy to reduce or eliminate entry barriers to markets, to make markets more contestable and to get rid of the costs of complying with unnecessary regulations

If successful, through incentivising economic agents, supply-side policies may increase the potential output of the economy and improve the underlying trend rate of economic growth. An increase in the economy's potential output can be illustrated by a rightward shift in the economy's production possibility frontier. This is shown in the left-hand panel of Figure 21. An improvement in the economy's underlying trend rate of growth can be illustrated by an increase in the slope or gradient of the trend output line shown in the right-hand panel of the same diagram.

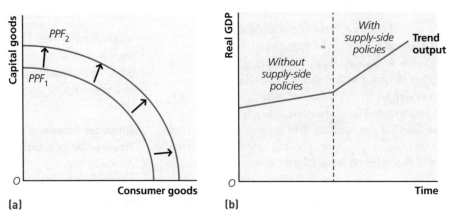

Figure 21 Economic growth illustrated by a rightward movement of the economy's *PPF* curve and by a steeper trend output line

There is little evidence, however, that in the UK pro-free-market supply-side policies have achieved the objective of increasing the trend growth rate, which has remained around 2.0% to 2.5% a year both before and after the implementation of supply-side policies from the 1980s onward.

How supply-side policies can affect unemployment, the rate of change of prices and UK external performance

By enabling output to grow more quickly, supply-side policies increase the demand for labour to produce the extra output, which reduces unemployment. And as we explain in the next section, successful supply-side policies can reduce the natural rate of unemployment (NRU).

Supporters of the use of pro-free-market supply-side policies argue that by reducing business's costs of production and by reducing monopoly profits through making markets more price competitive, supply-side policies reduce cost-push inflationary pressures. Also, by enabling productive capacity to grow in line with aggregate demand, successful supply-side policies help to reduce demand-pull inflationary pressures.

By creating 'lean and fit' firms, successful supply-side policies and supply-side reforms are also likely to improve the country's quality competitiveness. Taken together, increased price and quality competitiveness give the country a competitive edge, in both domestic and overseas markets. By improving both price and quality competitiveness, supply-side policies and supply-side reforms within the private sector can contribute to 'export-led' growth — though there is precious little evidence of this taking place in the UK.

The role of supply-side policies in reducing the natural rate of unemployment

The upper panel of Figure 22 depicts the economy's aggregate labour market, while the lower panel shows the long-run vertical Phillips curve and the natural rate of unemployment (NRU). As the upper panel shows, the natural or 'equilibrium' level of employment E_{N1} is determined in the economy's aggregate labour market at real wage rate w_{FE}. When the labour market is in equilibrium, the number of workers willing to work equals the number of workers whom firms wish to hire. The lower panel of the diagram shows the natural *level* of unemployment U_{N1} (or natural rate if stated as a percentage of the labour force) immediately below E_{N1} in the upper panel.

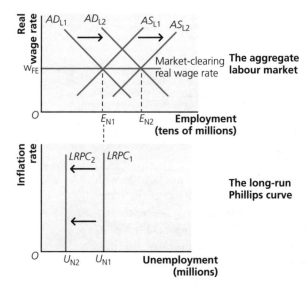

Figure 22 Bringing together the natural levels of employment and unemployment, labour market equilibrium and the long-run Phillips curve

According to the supply-side view, tax cuts can affect the natural levels and rates of employment and unemployment in the economy. Suppose, for example, that the government cuts employers' national insurance contributions. Employment costs fall, so it becomes more attractive for firms to employ labour. As a result, in the upper panel of Figure 22, the aggregate demand for labour curve shifts rightward from AD_{L1} to AD_{L2}. Likewise, if income tax is cut, this will increase workers' disposable income and thus the incentive to work, shifting the aggregate supply curve of labour rightward from AS_{L1} to AS_{L2}. Both these changes increase the economy's natural level of employment, which rises from E_{N1} to E_{N2}.

In the lower panel of Figure 22, the long-run Phillips curve shifts leftward from $LRPC_1$ to $LRPC_2$, which means that the economy's natural level of unemployment falls from U_{N1} to U_{N2}.

Free-market supply-side policies

Free-market supply-side policies include measures such as: tax cuts, privatisation, deregulation and some labour market reforms. Free-market economists believe that high rates of income tax and the overall burden on taxpayers create disincentives which, by reducing national income as taxation increases, also reduce the government's total tax revenue. This effect is illustrated by the Laffer curve in Figure 23. According to the diagram, if tax rates are currently above 50%, tax reductions towards 50% can not only free resources for the private sector to use, but also increase the government's total tax revenue.

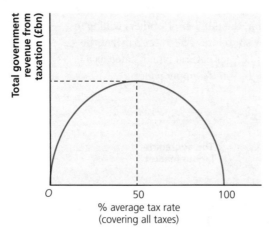

Figure 23 A Laffer curve

Free-market supply-side policies aim to replace public sector economic activity with that undertaken in the private sector, which reduces the economic role of the state. Privatisation shifts ownership of industries and firms from the public sector to the private sector. Pro-free-market labour market reforms reduce the power of trade unions and their legal protection, and also their power to bargain over pay. Taken together, deregulation and labour market reforms 'free up' markets.

Interventionist supply-side policies

These include measures such as government spending on education and training, industrial and regional policy, spending on infrastructure such as motorways, and subsidising spending on research and development (R&D). Interventionist supply-side policies are based on the view that government intervention in the economy is needed to correct market failure and short-termism, which may reduce investment and growth, whereas more recent pro-free-market supply-side policies have generally aimed to correct and reduce government failure.

Recent interventionist supply-side policies have included public sector investment in high-speed rail links between London, Birmingham and the north, together with George Osborne's plan, announced in 2014, to transform the north of England into an economic 'powerhouse' with investment of up to £15 billion to finance the building of infrastructure.

Supply-side policies can have microeconomic as well as macroeconomic effects

Supply-side fiscal policy, more often than not, aims to make markets and firms function better at the microeconomic level. The same is true for many other supply-side policies such as privatisation, deregulation and marketisation. The latter replaces non-market provision of goods and services such as education and healthcare with market provision, in which prices are charged.

Examination skills

The skills most likely to be tested by data-response and essay questions on *fiscal policy and supply-side policies* at A-level are as follows:

- Displaying knowledge of the structures of public spending and taxation in the UK
- Applying *AD/AS* analysis to explain fiscal and supply-side policy issues
- Ability to distinguish between demand-side and supply-side fiscal policy
- Understanding the difference between pro-free-market (anti-interventionist) and interventionist supply-side policies

Examination questions

Examination questions on *fiscal policy and supply-side policies* are likely to appear quite frequently in the Paper 2 and 3 exams. They can also be linked to *AD/AS* analysis, and fiscal policy and supply-side policies could also form a significant part of an answer to a generally worded question on other specification topics, such as *economic performance*. In the Questions & Answers section of this guide, your knowledge of fiscal policy is tested in DRQ 2 and in EQ 2. MCQ 12 is set on fiscal policy and supply-side policies.

Common examination errors

Commonly made mistakes on *fiscal policy and supply-side policies* include:

- assuming that fiscal policy always means demand management
- a lack of awareness of the supply-side elements of modern fiscal policy
- failing to understand interrelationships between fiscal policy and monetary policy
- a lack of a wider understanding of supply-side policies other than supply-side fiscal policy
- failing to appreciate the linkages between fiscal policy and topics such as market failures and income distribution

Summary

- Fiscal policy is the part of a government's economic policy aimed at achieving policy objectives through the use of the fiscal instruments.
- Fiscal policy instruments are taxation, public spending and the budget deficit or surplus.
- Demand-side fiscal policy, or Keynesian fiscal policy, manages aggregate demand.
- Along with other supply-side policies, supply-side fiscal policy aims to shift the *LRAS* curve to the right.
- Taxation is used to finance government spending, as is government borrowing.
- Progressive taxation and transfers of tax revenue to lower-income groups reduce income inequality, but may also adversely affect incentives.
- Supply-side fiscal policy tries to create incentives by cutting tax rates and making it less attractive to claim welfare benefits.
- Supply-side fiscal policy is often microeconomic rather than macroeconomic.

■ 4.2.6 The international economy

These notes relate to AQA specification section 4.2.6 and prepare you to answer examination questions on:

- globalisation
- trade
- the balance of payments
- exchange rate systems
- growth and development

Essential information

Globalisation

The causes of globalisation

Globalisation is the name given to the processes that integrate all or most of the world's economies, making countries increasingly dependent upon each other. Some economists argue that globalisation has occurred over centuries, going back at least as far as the creation of a system of relatively free worldwide trade in the nineteenth century.

Recent globalisation has been made possible by improvements in information and communication technology (ICT), as well as by developments in transport and other more traditional forms of technology. Examples of globalisation include service industries in the UK dealing with customers through call centres in India, and fashion companies designing their products in Europe, making them in south-east Asia and finally selling most of them in North America. The production of this Student Guide, being written in the UK and the USA, typeset in India, and printed in Italy, provides another example of globalisation.

Globalisation The process of growing economic integration of the world's economies.

The main characteristics of globalisation

Some of the main characteristics of globalisation are illustrated in Figure 24.

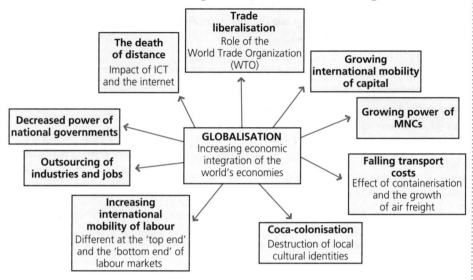

Figure 24 Characteristics of globalisation

These characteristics are:

- trade liberalisation — a process encouraged by the **World Trade Organization (WTO)**
- greater international mobility of capital and of labour
- a significant increase in the power of **multinational corporations (MNCs)**
- **deindustrialisation** of older industrial regions and countries, and the movement of manufacturing to **newly industrialising countries (NICs)**
- the movement to NICs of internationally mobile service industries, such as call centres and accounts offices
- a decrease in governmental power to influence decisions made by MNCs to shift economic activity between countries

The consequences of globalisation for less-developed and for more-developed countries

Less-developed countries are countries whose state of economic development is characterised by low national income per head, a high rate of population growth, low levels of **human capital**, high unemployment, poor **infrastructure** and overdependence on the export of a few primary commodities.

> **Less-developed countries** Countries considered behind in terms of their economy, human capital, infrastructure and industrial base.

> **Infrastructure** The result of past investment in buildings, roads, bridges, power supplies, fast broadband and other fixed capital goods that are needed for the economy to operate efficiently.

> **Human capital** The accumulated stock of skills and knowledge, relevant to work, embodied in human beings.

World Trade Organization (WTO) An international body whose purpose is to promote free trade by persuading countries to abolish barriers to trade.

Multinational corporations (MNCs) Businesses which own and operate subsidiary companies in countries other than where their headquarters are located.

Deindustrialisation The decline of manufacturing, often associated with its movement to other countries.

Newly industrialising countries (NICs) Countries with a growing industrial or manufacturing sector.

It is impossible in the limited space of a short Student Guide to do any sort of justice to this topic. But here are a few of the arguments you may develop and use:

- Supporters of the need for further globalisation believe that it has been the main force in improving production and living standards throughout the world, in less-developed countries as well as in more-developed countries.
- Particularly important in this process have been the benefits achieved from freer trade and much-reduced transport costs, and from the export of technological know-how from rich to poorer countries.
- These factors have contributed to the beginning of a shift of economic power away from **more-developed countries** to less-developed countries.
- On the debit side, less-developed countries have suffered from certain aspects of 'gung-ho capitalism', such as the spread of sweatshop factories and financial instability. But on the plus side, 'first-world' companies operating in less-developed countries have generally lifted living standards and acted as an engine for economic growth and development.
- Finally, globalisation has worked best for rich and poor countries alike when its main element has been an active 'pull-up strategy' rather than a mechanism for economic exploitation and social disruption.

The role of multinational corporations in globalisation

Traditionally, the headquarters of MNCs were almost always in developed countries such as the USA, the UK, Japan, Germany and France. However, a relatively recent development has been the emergence of MNCs based in countries such as India, China and Indonesia. The Indian company Tata, which owns Jaguar and Land Rover plants in the UK, and which recently owned most of the UK steel industry, provides a good example. Related to this growth of MNCs with headquarters in developing countries, have been decisions — either threatened or undertaken — by corporations such as the HSBC bank, for tax reasons, to move their headquarters to new locations, often in the developing world.

Trade

Absolute advantage and comparative advantage

At the heart of international trade theory is the model of **comparative advantage**. However, before we explain comparative advantage, we shall first explain the rather similar-sounding concept of **absolute advantage**. If a country is best at (or technically and productively most efficient at) producing a good or service, it possesses an absolute advantage in the good's production. Comparative advantage is measured in terms of *opportunity cost*, or what a country gives up when it increases the output of an industry by one unit. Note that a country may possess a comparative advantage even if it suffers an absolute disadvantage in the good's production.

Other economic benefits of trade, such as the ability to exploit economies of scale and increased competition

International trade between open economies thus increases each country's production possibilities, and also its consumption possibilities. According to its advocates, free trade widens choice for both producers and consumers, and facilitates faster rates of economic growth. Also, the international division of labour and successful

More-developed countries Countries with a high degree of economic development, high average income per head, high standards of living, usually with service industries dominating manufacturing, and investment having taken place over many years in human capital and infrastructure.

Absolute advantage A country has an absolute advantage if it can produce more of a good than other countries from the same amount of resources.

Comparative advantage Measured in terms of opportunity cost. The country with the least opportunity cost when producing a good possesses a comparative advantage in that good.

Exam tip

Make sure you understand the principle of comparative advantage, which is the key concept relating to international trade and specialisation.

specialisation reduce costs of production, and contribute to the widening of production and consumption possibilities.

If we lived in a **closed economy**, which is an economy without any international trade, the goods and services we could consume would be limited to those which the country's resource base allowed it to produce. In a small country, average costs of production are likely to be high because small population size and the absence of export markets mean that economies of scale and long production runs cannot be achieved.

By contrast, a country which is open to international trade (an **open economy**) can import raw materials and energy from the rest of the world. This widens the economy's production possibilities — though, in practice, open economies concentrate on producing the goods and services that they are competitive in producing, and import other goods and services. By exporting the goods they can produce competitively, open economies benefit from economies of scale and long production runs gained from access to the much larger world market. Likewise, imports lead to a vast array of choice and the possibility of a much higher level of economic welfare and living standards than is possible in a world without trade.

The costs of international trade

In addition to the freight and transport costs which result from international trade (though these have been reduced by the development of containerisation), international trade imposes other costs on countries. Even if the world as a whole benefits from the extension of free trade, trade sometimes imposes costs on particular firms and producers. An obvious example occurs when firms and industries collapse in the face of international competition. In the UK, for example, much of the market-gardening industry has collapsed because the farmers involved cannot compete with flowers and vegetables grown in subtropical and tropical regions and then air-freighted into the UK market. On the other hand, for farmers in the developing world who sell their produce in the UK market, overspecialisation can result in monoculture or the growing of a single cash crop for export. Monoculture often leads to soil erosion, vulnerability to pests and falling future agricultural yields. The resulting decreasing returns to scale suffered by farmers who overspecialise weakens the case for complete specialisation and free trade.

The reasons for changes in the pattern of trade between the UK and the rest of the world

In recent decades, the pattern of world trade has become quite different from the North–South exchange of manufactured goods for primary products that previously characterised world trade. In the new North–North pattern of trade, the developed industrial economies now exchange goods and services mostly with each other. However, a growing fraction of their trade, particularly in the case of imports, is with newly industrialising countries (NICs) or emerging markets, particularly India, China and South Korea.

The shift of manufacturing to China and other NICs reflects changing competitive and comparative advantage and the deindustrialisation of the UK, North America and some of the major European economies. Only a relatively small proportion of the trade of North countries is with poorer countries in the non-oil-producing developing world.

Closed economy An economy not open to international trade.

Open economy An economy open to international trade.

However, 'other developing countries' include emerging-market 'giants' such as India and China, the latter having become the world's largest exporter of manufactured goods to developed economies such as the UK. The growing importance of emerging market countries, particularly China, in international trade explains why the share of their trade in UK imports and exports has been creeping upward.

The nature of protectionist policies, such as: tariffs, quotas and export subsidies

Protectionist policies involve import and export controls. These can be divided into quantity controls such as an import quota, which puts a maximum limit on imports, and tariffs (import duties) and their opposite, export subsidies, which respectively raise the price of imports and reduce the price of exports.

The causes and consequences of countries adopting protectionist policies

Countries adopt protectionist policies for a number of reasons. These include:

- to protect infant industries — recently established industries in developing countries
- to protect sunset industries — industries such as steel which are in decline in already developed countries

The infant and sunset industry arguments are closely related to strategic trade theory, which has grown in influence in recent years. The theory attempts to justify governments creating competitive advantage by nurturing strategically selected industries or economic sectors. However, economists who believe in the virtues of free trade argue that, by raising prices and reducing trade, protectionism leads to an inefficient allocation of resources.

The main features of a customs union

There are a number of different trading blocs such as customs unions and free trade areas, which display similarities but also differences. A customs union and a free trade area are similar in that both organisations have internal free trade between member states. However, the difference lies in the way tariffs are set against imports from non-member states. Members of a free trade area are free to set their own tariffs against non-members, but members of a customs union lose this freedom and have to abide by an external tariff common to all member states.

The main characteristics of the Single European Market (SEM)

The European Union (EU), or European Economic Community (EEC) as it then was called, started life in 1958 as a customs union. It created free trade in goods, but not in services, and did not allow the free movement of capital and labour. However, the intention was for the customs union to develop into a full common market in goods, services, capital and labour. This was largely achieved when the Single European Market (SEM) came into operation in 1993, having earlier been passed into UK law in the 1987 Single European Act.

> Single European Market (SEM) The SEM came into existence in 1993 in an attempt to establish the 'four freedoms' — free movement of goods, services, workers and capital — between the EU member states.

Quota A physical limit on the quantities of imported goods allowed into a country.

Tariffs Taxes imposed on imports from other countries entering a country. Also known as import duties.

Export subsidies Money given to domestic firms by the government to encourage firms to sell their products abroad and to help make their goods cheaper in export markets.

Knowledge check 12

Why has the growth of China's trade been used to justify protectionism?

Customs union A trading bloc in which member countries enjoy internal free trade in goods and possibly services, with all the member countries protected by a common external tariff barrier.

European Union (EU) An economic and partially political union established in 1993 after the ratification of the Maastricht Treaty by members of the European Community and since expanded to include numerous central and eastern European nations.

The SEM's main achievements have been:

- abolishing trade barriers and physical customs controls
- harmonising national rules preventing companies trading across borders
- changing public procurement rules such as how public sector bodies like the NHS order services, across the EU
- modifying legislation to allow EU citizens to move to and work in other member states
- removing barriers to the services sector and allowing companies to provide cross-border services, at least according to supporters of the EU

All these help to ensure that market liberalisation benefits as many EU businesses and consumers as possible, again according to supporters of the EU.

The consequences for the UK of its membership of the European Union (EU)

One way of assessing the consequences for the UK of its membership of the European Union is to answer the question: has EU membership been *trade creating* or *trade diverting*?

Trade creation increases the total volume of international trade because the growth of internal free trade among members exceeds any loss of trade with non-members brought about by tariffs protecting the trading bloc. After the formation of a customs union, member states can import lower-cost products from other member states, rather than producing the products themselves at a higher cost. This leads to efficiency gains.

Trade diversion, by contrast, refers to changes in the pattern of international trade which occur when trade that used to take place with non-member states diverts into trade between member states. If, after the formation of a customs union, a member country replaces imported goods from lower-cost countries in the rest of the world with goods produced by higher-cost member countries, efficiency losses occur.

We can also ask: has there been an increase in **foreign direct investment (FDI)** into the UK economy as a result of membership of the EU?

The role of the World Trade Organization (WTO)

The World Trade Organization (WTO) is the only global international organisation dealing with the rules of trade between nations. At its heart are the WTO agreements, negotiated and signed by the bulk of the world's trading nations and ratified in their parliaments. The goal is to help producers of goods and services, exporters and importers conduct their business.

Besides administering its trade agreements, the WTO's role involves handling trade disputes, monitoring national trade policies, providing technical assistance and training for developing countries, and cooperation with other international organisations such as the IMF and the World Bank.

The WTO agreements cover goods, services and intellectual property. They spell out the principles of liberalisation, and the permitted exceptions. They include individual countries' commitments to lower customs tariffs and other trade barriers, and to open and keep open services markets.

> **Exam tip**
>
> Future exam questions may ask about the possible impact of the British referendum result in favour of the UK leaving the EU (Brexit).

> **Foreign direct investment (FDI)** Spending of funds overseas on capital assets, such as manufacturing and service industry capacity, by a business with headquarters in another country.

Content Guidance

The balance of payments

The balance of payments measures all the currency flows into and out of a country in a particular time period, e.g. a year.

The difference between the current, capital and financial accounts on the balance of payments

The main items in the UK's balance of payments in 2015 are shown in Table 2.

Table 2 Selected items from the UK balance of payments, 2015 (£m)

The current account (mostly trade flows)	
Balance of trade in goods	−125,350
Balance of trade in services	+88,677
Net primary income flows	−34,775
Net secondary income flows	−24,779
Balance of payments on the current account	**−96,227**
The capital account (transfers, which used to be in the current account)	**−1,101**
The financial account (capital flows, which used to be in the capital account)	
Net direct investment	−66,092
Net portfolio investment	−269,272
Other capital flows (mostly short-term 'hot money' flows)	+220,506
Changes in reserves	+21,079
Financial account balance	**−93,779**
The balance (errors and omissions)	**+3,549**

Source: ONS, Statistical Bulletin: Balance of Payments: Oct to Dec and annual 2015, 31 March 2016

For the most part, the balance of payments on current account measures the flow of expenditure on goods and services, and shows the difference between the amount received from exports and the amount paid for imports.

Several years ago, a change was made to the way the UK balance of payments is presented. The items in the capital account, a long-standing part of the balance of payments, were changed. Flows of investment spending were moved out of the capital account and listed under a new heading: the financial account. The capital account now comprises various transfers of income that were part of the current account before the new method of classification was adopted.

The current account comprises trade in goods, trade in services, primary income and secondary income

The current account, which is explained in some detail on pages 35 to 37 in *Student Guide 2*, is usually regarded as the most important part of the balance of payments because it reflects the economy's international competitiveness and the extent to which the country may or may not be living within its means.

The main items in the current account are the balance of trade in goods and the balance of trade in services. The other two items in the current account are primary and secondary income flows. Net primary income flows are profits flowing into the UK, generated by UK-owned assets which are located in other countries, minus

Balance of payments on current account The sum of the balance of trade (goods and services exports less imports), net primary income (including investment income) and net secondary income (including current transfers).

Capital account The part of the balance of payments which includes capital transfers and the net acquisition or disposal of non-produced, non-financial assets.

Financial account The part of the balance of payments which records capital flows into and out of the economy.

Primary income flows Profits, dividends and interest payments flowing between countries.

profits flowing out of the UK, generated by overseas-owned assets which are located in the UK. Secondary income flows are current transfers of income arising from such items as gifts between residents of different countries, donations to charities abroad, and overseas aid. The UK's net contribution to the EU budget is another example of a current transfer of income between countries, though this may soon disappear.

The meaning of a deficit and a surplus on the current account

A current account deficit occurs whenever, taken together, payments for trade in goods, trade in services, and primary and secondary income, flowing out of the economy, are greater than the corresponding inflows. Similarly, a surplus on current account occurs whenever, taken together, payments for trade in goods, trade in services, and primary and secondary income, flowing into the economy, are greater than the corresponding outflows.

Table 2 shows that when the first estimates of the UK balance of payments for 2015 were published in March 2016, the current account was in deficit to the tune of £96,227 million. Nested within the overall deficit, the balance of trade in services ran a surplus of £88,677 million, but this was more than countered by a balance of trade deficit in goods of £125,350 million. At the time, this was the largest ever recorded deficit in the UK's trade in goods, though given the fact that the deficit has since continued to grow, it reflects the UK's lack of competitiveness in international markets for goods.

The factors that influence a country's current account balance

As indicated above, international competitiveness is a main factor influencing whether or not the balances of trade in goods and services are in deficit or surplus. A fall in the exchange rate increases the price competitiveness of exports. Conversely, a rising exchange rate reduces price competitiveness. An increase in productivity makes goods cheaper to produce, which increases their price competitiveness. Productivity also affects quality competitiveness, via the effect of investment in new capital goods. Not only may a high investment rate increase labour productivity by combining workers with more capital per head, it also usually equips them with better quality and 'state-of-the art' capital, which makes the country's goods more attractive in world markets. Comparative rates of inflation also influence price competitiveness. A domestic inflation rate which is lower than the inflation rate in competitor countries increases the price competitiveness of the country's exports.

As we explain in the next section, when UK-based multinational companies invest in capital assets located in other countries, the profit income generated from overseas investment flows back to the parent company and its UK shareholders. The investment itself is an outward capital flow, but the income it generates is current income, figuring in the current account of the balance of payments. Until recently, much more investment income flowed into the UK than flowed out. However, the pattern of these flows has reversed, and the outward primary income flow (according to Table 2, a £24,799 million outflow in 2015) has been a major cause of the UK's growing current account deficit.

The consequences of investment flows between countries

Within the financial account of the balance of payments, we distinguish between long-term direct capital flows, long-term portfolio capital flows, and short-term

Secondary income flows Current transfers, such as gifts of money, international aid and transfers between the UK and the EU, flowing into or out of the UK economy in a particular year.

Knowledge check 13

Should a large balance of payments surplus on current account be regarded as bad?

Capital flows Overseas investment in physical assets in the case of direct capital flows (foreign direct investment) and financial assets in the case of long-term portfolio investment and short-term 'hot money' investment.

speculative 'hot money' capital flows. Direct overseas investment involves acquisition of real productive assets, such as factories, located in other countries. These flows are a response to people's decisions to invest in economic activities and industries located in countries that have a competitive advantage. But since changes in competitive advantage usually take place quite slowly, long-term direct capital flows tend to be relatively stable and predictable.

By contrast, portfolio investment flows involve the purchase of financial assets (that is, pieces of paper laying claim to the ownership of real assets) rather than physical or directly productive assets.

Lastly, short-term capital movements, which are also called 'hot money' flows, are largely speculative. The flows occur because the owners of funds, which include companies and banks as well as wealthy private individuals, believe that a quick speculative profit can be made by moving funds between currencies. Speculating that a currency's exchange rate is about to rise, owners of funds move money into that currency and out of other currencies whose exchange rates are expected to fall.

The policies that might be used to correct a balance of payments deficit or surplus

Traditionally, it was thought that a government (or its central bank) can use three different policies to try to cure a persistent deficit caused by an overvalued exchange rate. These are the '3 Ds' of deflation, direct controls (imposing import controls), and **devaluation** or currency depreciation, which are described in the next section. In a similar way, the '3 Rs' of **reflation**, **revaluation** and the removal of import controls can be used to try to reduce or eliminate a persistent balance of payments surplus on current account.

It is now generally agreed, however, that although deflation, devaluation and direct controls may be effective *short-term* policies for reducing current account deficits, *long-term* improvement in trade flows requires appropriate and successful supply-side policies and supply-side reforms undertaken by firms within the economy.

Expenditure-switching and expenditure-reducing policies

As Figure 25 indicates, a deflationary policy used to try to reduce a current account deficit is an **expenditure-reducing policy**. However, devaluation of the exchange rate is an **expenditure-switching policy**, as is the imposition of import controls.

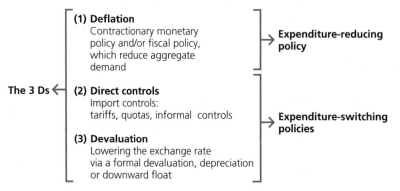

Figure 25 Expenditure-reducing and expenditure-switching policies

> **Devaluation** Central bank's decision to reduce an adjustable-peg exchange rate, or more loosely a downward float of the exchange rate.
>
> **Reflation** A persistent and continuing tendency for real output to increase. A reflationary policy such as expansionary fiscal or monetary policy increases aggregate demand.
>
> **Revaluation** Central bank's decision to raise an adjustable-peg exchange rate, or more loosely an upward float of the exchange rate.
>
> **Expenditure-reducing policy** Government policy which aims to reduce a current account deficit by reducing the demand for imports by reducing the level of aggregate demand in the economy.
>
> **Expenditure-switching policy** Government policy which aims to eliminate a current account deficit by switching domestic demand away from imports to domestically produced goods.

The effect that policies used to correct a current account deficit may have on other macroeconomic policy objectives

We mentioned on page 9 that a policy conflict may exist between deflating aggregate demand to reduce a current account deficit and achieving the macroeconomic policy objectives of economic growth and low unemployment. In essence, deflation attempts to achieve the *external* policy objective of a satisfactory balance of payments on current account at the expense of domestic policy objectives which increase people's welfare and living standards. In contrast, by increasing the prices of imported goods and services, an expenditure-switching devaluation of the exchange rate is likely to conflict with the control of inflation policy objective.

The significance of deficits and surpluses for an individual economy

While a short-run deficit or surplus on current account does not pose a problem, a persistent or long-run imbalance indicates fundamental disequilibrium. Although in the short run a deficit allows a country's residents to enjoy living standards boosted by imports, and thus higher than would be possible from the consumption of the country's output alone, in the long run, the decline of the country's industries in the face of international competition lowers living standards.

While many people agree that a persistent current account deficit can pose serious problems, few realise that a balance of payments surplus on current account can also lead to problems. Although a small surplus may be a justifiable objective of government policy, a large payments surplus should be regarded as undesirable. This is because the balance of payments must balance for the world as a whole. It is therefore impossible for all countries to run surpluses simultaneously. Unless countries with persistently large surpluses agree to take action to reduce their surpluses, deficit countries cannot reduce their deficits. Also, as it leads to an injection of aggregate demand into the circular flow of income, a balance of payments surplus can be inflationary.

Exchange rate systems

How exchange rates are determined in freely floating exchange rate systems

Exchange rates and a foreign exchange market exist because different countries use different currencies to pay for international trade. A currency's exchange rate is simply its external price, expressed in terms of another currency such as the US dollar, or gold, or indeed in terms of an artificial unit such as the sterling index, which is the weighted average of a sample of exchange rates of countries with which the UK trades.

With freely floating (cleanly floating) exchange rates, the external value of a country's currency is determined on foreign exchange markets by the forces of demand and supply alone. Figure 26 illustrates how both the exchange rate and the current account of the balance of payments are determined in a freely floating system — subject to the very artificial assumption that there are no capital flows. If demand for pounds is D and supply is S_1, the equilibrium exchange rate, expressed against the US dollar, is $1.50. Assuming exports and imports are the only items in the current account of the balance of payments, the current account is also in equilibrium.

The value of exports equalling the value of imports is £10 billion at the equilibrium exchange rate. When there are no capital flows, exchange rate equilibrium implies balance of payments equilibrium on the current account and vice versa.

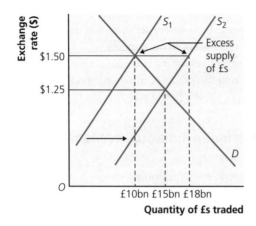

Figure 26 Exchange rate determination on a freely floating exchange rate system

Suppose that some event or shock disturbs this initial equilibrium — for example, an improvement in the quality of foreign-produced goods causing UK residents to increase their demand for imports at all existing sterling prices. Because the demand for foreign exchange to pay for imports increases, the supply curve of pounds shifts to the right from S_1 to S_2. At the exchange rate of $1.50, the current account is in deficit by £8 billion, which is also the excess supply of pounds on the foreign exchange market.

The market mechanism now swings into action to eliminate this excess supply, thereby restoring equilibrium, both for the exchange rate and for the current account. The selling of pounds to get rid of excess supply causes the exchange rate to fall, which increases the price competitiveness of British exports and reduces that of imports. The adjustment process continues until a new equilibrium exchange rate is reached at $1.25 to the pound, with exports and imports both equalling £15 billion.

How governments can intervene to influence the exchange rate

There are two main ways in which a government, or more usually its central bank, can intervene in foreign exchange markets to influence the exchange rate. The first is by buying or selling its own currency on the foreign exchange market. If the exchange rate threatens to rise above a particular level, the central bank sells its own currency on the foreign exchange market to offset excess demand for the currency that would otherwise pull up the exchange rate. Likewise, if the exchange rate threatens to fall below the central bank's target rate, the bank steps into the foreign exchange market and buys its own currency.

The second method a central bank can use to support its target exchange rate is by changing domestic interest rates within the economy. In the case of the pound, lower domestic interest rates might cause international holders of the pound to sell pounds and buy other currencies. This would cause the pound's exchange rate to fall. Conversely, an increase in UK interest rates attracts 'hot money' into the pound.

> **Exam tip**
>
> Exam questions are usually set on floating exchange rates, though questions on fixed exchange rates are also possible.

Through the selling of other currencies and the buying of the pound, short-run capital inflows raise the demand for pounds and prop up its exchange rate.

The advantages and disadvantages of floating and fixed exchange rate systems

With regard to the advantages of a *floating* exchange rate, domestic monetary policy can be completely independent of external conditions and influences. The country is free to pursue an independent monetary policy aimed at achieving purely domestic economic objectives, without the need to assign monetary policy and interest rates to support the exchange rate or to attract capital flows into the country to finance a current account deficit.

Freely floating exchange rates nevertheless have some disadvantages, particularly relating to the fact that in the modern globalised world in which financial capital is internationally mobile, capital flows rather than exports and imports are the main determinants of floating exchange rates. The argument that a freely floating exchange rate can never be overvalued or undervalued for very long depends crucially on the assumption that speculation and capital flows have no influence on exchange rates. This assumption is wrong. Exchange rates, freely floating and fixed, have become extremely vulnerable to speculative capital or 'hot money' movements. A massive inward capital flow can overvalue an exchange rate and create a serious deficit on the current account.

A further disadvantage is that a floating exchange rate may unleash a vicious spiral of ever-faster inflation and exchange rate depreciation. Rising import prices caused by a falling exchange rate cause the domestic inflation rate to increase, which erodes the export competitiveness won by the initial depreciation of the exchange rate. A further fall in the exchange rate is then required to recover the lost advantage — and so on.

Arguably, the main advantages of *fixed* exchange rates are: certainty and stability; and the anti-inflationary discipline they impose on a country's domestic economic management and on the behaviour of its workers and firms.

The disadvantages are: a possible increase in uncertainty, which can disrupt the economy if devaluation or revaluation is expected; continuing overvaluation or undervaluation of the currency, leading to resource misallocation; severe deflationary costs of lost output and unemployment for a deficit country and the importing of inflation by a surplus country; possible recurrent balance of payments or currency crises in a country whose currency is overvalued; and the tying up of resources in official reserves (needed to support the fixed exchange rate), which could be used more productively elsewhere.

Advantages and disadvantages for a country of joining a currency union such as the eurozone

If several countries form a currency union and use the same currency, their inhabitants will benefit from efficiency gains. They no longer have to worry about possible future changes in exchange rates, and the costs involved in currency conversion. These gains will be greater the more economically interconnected the countries are, in terms of their trading relationship, the freedom of labour and capital to move between countries, and a unified fiscal policy covering all member countries.

Eurozone The name used for the group of EU countries that have replaced their national currencies with the euro. In 2016, 19 of the then 28 EU countries were in the eurozone, though this may change in future years. The eurozone is also known as the euro area.

Currency union An agreement between a group of countries to share a common currency, and usually to have a single monetary and foreign exchange rate policy.

In these circumstances, the advantages of adopting a common currency can lead to benefits for all the member states within the currency union.

However, for the benefits to be realised, there must be a common fiscal policy, which provides a mechanism for transferring resources — for example, in the form of subsidies or lower tax rates — from the more prosperous parts of the currency union to the less prosperous countries. This is what happens in the UK, for example, when taxes paid by Londoners are directed into public spending projects in Scotland, Wales and Northern Ireland. The UK and the USA are successful common currency areas, but the eurozone is much less successful. The eurozone lacks such a common fiscal policy and is not an optimal currency area. This has led to the economic problems suffered by eurozone countries.

Growth and development

The difference between growth and development

Economic growth measures changes in the real *quantity* of goods and services that an economy actually produces, or has the potential to produce. Economic development goes further, encompassing not just the increase in quantity of output, but also its *quality* and contribution to human happiness or economic welfare.

Economic development can be measured by:

- a general improvement in living standards which reduces poverty and human suffering
- access to resources such as food and housing that are required to satisfy basic human needs
- access to opportunities for human development (for example, through education and training)
- sustainability and regeneration, through reducing resource depletion and degradation
- access to decent healthcare

The main characteristics of less-developed economies

The term 'less-developed economies' covers a wide range of economies, from the extremely poor to what the United Nations (UN) calls higher middle-income economies. There are various ways of identifying the main characteristics of less-developed economies, though these will differ in their significance when comparing, for example, a largely pre-industrial economy where most of the population are engaged in subsistence agriculture with the slum dwellers of densely populated areas which are becoming characteristic of increasingly urbanised developing countries.

However, some of the characteristics evident in most less-developed countries are:

- low levels of GDP per capita and the low living standard of many in the population
- great inequalities of income and wealth
- a high birth rate and a relatively high death rate
- a fast rate of growth of population combined with a low life expectancy
- high levels of poverty
- a low proportion of the population enrolled in education
- poor health due to poor nutrition, and lack of access to facilities such as clean water and proper sanitation

> **Exam tip**
>
> The difference between economic growth and economic development is likely to appear in exam questions in Papers 2 and 3.

- poor provision of healthcare
- economies dependent on primary product production combined with rapid growth of urban areas and shanty towns
- in the towns, a high dependency ratio of young and old relative to adults in formal jobs

Indicators of development

Economists usually use GDP per capita as their first indicator of economic development. Unfortunately, for most poor developing countries, GDP is usually greater than another national income indicator of development, gross national income or GNI. Profit outflows and interest payments out of developing economies to more-developed economies, and to banks within these economies, explain why this is the case.

These days, the United Nations **Human Development Index (HDI)** is generally preferred to conventional national income figures to show developments in economic welfare. The HDI is constructed by measuring life expectancy at birth, mean years of schooling and expected years of schooling, and GNI per head of population, reflecting purchasing power parity (PPP) in US dollars. The maximum value of the HDI is 1 (or unity). The closer a country's HDI is to 1, then the greater its human development, measured in terms of the three indicators specified in the index.

Factors that affect growth and development

Although there are a large number of factors which affect growth and development, here we mention just two — investment in physical capital and investment in human capital.

- Investment in physical capital involves the purchase of new capital goods. While being a component of aggregate demand, which, when it increases, shifts the *AD* curve to the right, investment also affects aggregate supply. Together with technical progress, investment is one of the 'engines' of economic growth, shifting rightward an economy's production possibility frontier and also its *LRAS* curve. The economic growth that results *enables* economic development to occur, though it does not guarantee that development takes place.
- Investment in human capital, or investment in education and training which increases labour productivity, is also usually an important part of both growth and economic development.

Barriers to growth and development

There are, of course, many barriers which prevent or reduce economic growth, and with it the chance for further economic development. Five of these are corruption, institutional factors, infrastructure, inadequate human capital and a lack of **property rights**.

- Corruption and bribery, which are often endemic features of life in poor countries, but also in richer countries such as Russia, divert scarce resources away from more productive uses to protect less efficient resource use. Production costs and consumer prices also rise — for example through 'backhanders' paid by customers to corrupt officials and to employees of firms with which they wish to do business.
- Institutional factors, which can differ greatly between less-developed and more-developed economies, include countries' legal and judicial structures, public

Human Development Index (HDI) Uses life expectancy at birth, mean years of schooling and expected years of schooling, and gross national income per head of population to measure economic development in different countries.

Property rights A property right is the exclusive authority to determine how a resource is used, whether that resource is owned by government or by individuals.

administration systems, the availability of, and access to, financial institutions such as banks and capital markets, the role, if any, of the civil service, attitudes to work, and the education and training systems. An efficient, policed and enforced 'law of contract' should be viewed as a necessary condition for businesses and consumers to 'do business with each other'. For example, without an enforced law of contract, firms may end up not supplying goods or services to consumers and other firms, even though the goods or services have been paid for. In this situation, business transactions may simply not take place.

- It goes almost without saying that rich countries, in the course of their development over decades (and sometimes centuries), have built up an infrastructure of roads, railways, and telephone and communication networks, together with other key elements of a modern economy. Poorer developing countries lack such infrastructure, which is an important factor holding back their development.

- Investment in human capital can be as important as investment in physical capital goods such as machinery if long-run economic growth and development are to take place. Human capital embodies the accumulated stock of skills and knowledge that are relevant to employment.

- Traditional, more or less undeveloped societies often lack private property rights. Most resources are communally owned. While to some this represents an idyllic paradise economy, to others it is a major cause of a lack of economic development. The establishment of, and ability to trade in, private property rights is regarded by many as a necessary pre-condition for successful economic development.

Policies that might be adopted to promote economic growth and development

Appropriate policies for promoting economic growth and development include the standard macroeconomic government policies explained in earlier topics. These include demand-side fiscal policy and monetary policy and supply-side policies, all of which can be focused on achieving economic growth and development and overall economic stability.

Also important are appropriate microeconomic policies which aim to reduce or correct the various market failures that growth may bring about. These can include the use of taxes and subsidies, respectively, to punish or deter the production of negative externalities and demerit goods, and to encourage the production necessary to narrow unjustifiable inequalities in the distributions of income and wealth. However, such policies may harm the incentives provided by markets that many think are essential for sustained growth and development.

Economists and politicians sometimes argue that a higher level of state intervention is required to bring about growth and development in poor countries than in more-developed economies. Believers in the virtues of free markets disagree, citing the many cases of government failure that state intervention brings about. In recent decades, pro-free-market approaches have generally gained the upper hand, though not completely so. The strategic trade theory justification of a degree of protectionism in developing countries is a case in point. In practice, there is a strong case for combining market-based instruments with some forms of government intervention.

The role of aid and trade in promoting growth and development

Economists often debate the issue of whether **aid** is more important than trade (or vice versa) in promoting economic development. The orthodox view in countries such as the UK and the USA is that free trade and trade liberalisation are more important than aid in this respect. Free-market economists believe that international specialisation and complete free trade, undertaken in accordance with the principle of comparative advantage, benefit all the countries involved.

However, not all economists agree. The Korean economist Ha-Joon Chang has argued that governments in already developed economies are fully in favour of free trade — but only if their countries face little or no competition from developing economies. As soon as such competition emerges, the rich countries 'pull up the drawbridge', arguing that protectionism is necessary to protect themselves from the 'unfair' competition from cheap-labour countries. Rich countries also argue that they need protecting from countries in the much poorer developing world which steal their technology and clone their products, partly by ignoring international patent laws and other aspects of intellectual copyright. However, transfers of technology can be an important mechanism for stimulating the development of the world's less prosperous economies. Strategic trade theorists such as Paul Krugman have also argued that developing countries can speed up the pace of development by first selecting, and then protecting, key industries deemed vital for successful economic growth.

Having said this, there is plenty of evidence that the growth of free trade and improved transport links — brought about, for example, by the containerisation of cargo — have been major factors responsible for the huge growth in international trade over recent decades.

> **Aid** Money, goods and services and 'soft' loans given by the government of one country or a multilateral institution such as the World Bank to help another country. Non-government organisations (NGOs) such as Oxfam also provide aid.

> **Exam tip**
>
> The 'trade versus aid' issue is likely to appear in exam questions.

Examination skills

The skills most likely to be tested by data-response and essay questions on *the international economy* at A-level are as follows:

- Performing calculations, for example on comparative advantage, the balance of payments and changes in exchange rates
- Drawing accurate diagrams to show welfare gains and losses from trade and protectionism
- Displaying knowledge of patterns of world and UK trade, and recent changes in the balance of payments and exchange rates
- The ability to link exchange rates to monetary policy
- Understanding the difference between economic growth and economic development

Examination questions

Examination questions on *the international economy* are likely to focus on the causes and consequences of globalisation, the advantages and disadvantages of free trade, correction and reduction of balance of payments deficits on current account, the advantages and disadvantages of floating exchange rates, and economic development issues. MCQs 13, 14 and 15 in the Questions & Answers section of this guide are on trade and globalisation, the balance of payments and exchange rates, and economic development. The Context 1 data-response question focuses on economic growth in the so-called BRIC countries (Brazil, Russia, India and China). The title of Essay 3 is: The benefits and costs of globalisation. Finally, the investigation question is: Should there be a return to protectionism?

Common examination errors

Commonly made mistakes on *the international economy* include:

- confusing comparative advantage with absolute advantage
- failing to appreciate the limitations of the principle of comparative advantage
- assuming that free trade is advantageous for all countries, at all times
- confusing the current account of the balance of payments with capital flows
- confusing current account equilibrium with balance on the balance of payments
- failing to understand how a floating exchange rate may eliminate a current account deficit
- writing one-sided polemical essays for or against EMU, the euro and EU membership
- confusing economic growth and economic development

Summary

- Globalisation is the name given for the increasing integration of the world's economies.
- According to the principle of comparative advantage, specialisation and trade can lead to an increase in world output, which can translate into a net welfare gain.
- Import controls have been justified by strategic trade theory, the protection of infant industries and a variety of other economic and non-economic arguments.
- The balance of payments contains two main parts: the current account and the financial account.
- The expenditure-reducing policy of deflation and/or the expenditure-switching policies of import controls and devaluation can be used to reduce a current account deficit.

- An exchange rate is the external price of a currency in terms of another currency.
- Provided there are no capital flows, a freely floating exchange rate can eliminate a trade deficit or surplus.
- The advantages of a fixed exchange rate relate closely to the disadvantages of a floating rate.
- The euro has replaced national currencies for the majority of EU member states that are in the eurozone.
- Economic development is not the same as economic growth.
- Free-market economists generally argue that reducing barriers to international trade is more important than aid in promoting economic development.

Questions & Answers

A-level Paper 2

At A-level, Paper 2 'The national and international economy' is 2 hours long and has a maximum mark of 80. The exam paper contains two sections, A and B, both of which must be answered. Section A, which accounts for 40 marks (50% of the total), comprises two data-response questions (DRQs), labelled Context 1 and Context 2, of which you should answer one. Section B, which also accounts for 40 marks (50% of the total), contains three essay questions (EQs), of which you should answer one. Essays account for 50% of total assessment in the A-level Paper 1 and Paper 2 exams.

A-level Paper 3

Besides including a case study investigation, the A-level Paper 3 exam has 30 multiple-choice questions (MCQs), of which roughly half are on macroeconomics with the others on microeconomics. The MCQs that follow in this guide, which are all on macroeconomics, are similar to those in the A-level Paper 3 exam. The MCQs in Section A of Paper 3 are followed in Section B of Paper 3 by extended response questions based on a case study or investigation which require a student to draw together different areas of the specification. An 'extended response' is evidence generated by a student that is of sufficient length to allow that student to demonstrate the ability to construct and develop a sustained line of reasoning which is coherent, relevant, substantiated and logically structured. The case study in Part B is not pre-released.

The assessment objectives (AOs)

Assessment objectives are set by a government agency, Ofqual, and are the same across the AS and A-level economics specifications. The exams measure how students have achieved the following assessment objectives:

- AO1: Demonstrate knowledge of terms/concepts and theories/models to show an understanding of the behaviour of economic agents (consumers, workers and firms) and how they are affected by and respond to economic issues. Weighting: at A-level 20–23%.
- AO2: Apply knowledge and understanding to various economic contexts to show how economic agents are affected by and respond to economic issues. Weighting: at A-level 26–29%.
- AO3: Analyse issues within economics, showing an understanding of their impact on economic agents. Weighting: at A-level 26–29%.
- AO4: Evaluate economic arguments and use qualitative and quantitative evidence to support informed judgements relating to economic issues. Weighting: at A-level 22–25%.

AO1 and AO2 are testing 'lower-order' skills, whereas AO3 and AO4 test 'higher-order' skills.

A strategy for tackling the A-level papers

Paper 2 (and Paper 1)

1   On opening the examination booklet, skim-read all the data-response and essay questions, but don't at this stage read the data extracts in the Context questions (the data-response questions).

2   Read the questions in both Context 1 and 2 more fully, paying particular attention to the accessibility of the data and whether you can write a good answer to the final part of each question, the part that carries the most marks.

3   After careful thought, make your final choice and spend about 55 minutes answering all the parts of the context you choose. Take account of the marks indicated in brackets for each sub-question when allocating the 55 minutes between each part of the question. Make sure you spend over half the time answering the final part [04] or [08] of the question.

4   While answering the Context questions, you will have been thinking subconsciously about the three essay questions (EQs) you skim-read earlier. Again, you should choose the essay question primarily on the basis of the relative ease or difficulty of the second part of the three questions.

5   Again, take account of the marks indicated in brackets for each sub-question when allocating the 55 or so minutes between each part of the question. Make sure you spend over half the time answering the second part of the essay question.

6   For both your chosen questions, remember to obey the key instruction words at the beginning of each part of the question.

7   In the last 10 minutes of the examination, read through your written answers to your chosen questions, checking and correcting mistakes — including spelling and mistakes in the grammar.

Paper 3

1   Spend about 5 minutes skim-reading the case study in Part B and the three parts of the question which follow.

2   Then spend a maximum of 30 minutes (a minute per question) answering the 30 multiple-choice questions in Part A. While answering the MCQs, you will have been thinking subconsciously about the investigation question (IQ) you skim-read earlier.

3   Reread the Extracts in the case study in Part B, and then answer the three parts of the question, paying particular attention to interpreting the numerical data in the case study and to showing your evaluation skills. Remember, good economic analysis is a necessary first step to good evaluation.

4   If you have any time left, check your answers to the MCQs and read through your answers to the case study question.

The exam questions in this guide

This guide includes 21 examination-style questions designed to be a key learning, revision and exam preparation resource. We start off with 15 multiple-choice questions (MCQs), which reflects the fact that approximately half of the MCQs in Part A of Paper 3 at A-level are set on macroeconomic topics, with the remaining 15 being set on microeconomic topics, which are covered in *Study Guide 3*.

The MCQs are followed by two data-response questions (DRQs) and three essay questions (EQs). Each of these questions is similar to those set in A-level Paper 2. All the DRQs or Context questions contain three data extracts, which are followed by four sub-parts to the question: [01], [02], [03] and [04] for the Context 1 question and [05], [06], [07] and [08] for the Context 2 question. The maximum marks for each sub-part are [01] and [05]: 2 marks; [02] and [06]: 4 marks; [03] and [07]: 9 marks, and [04] and [08]: 25 marks.

Part B of Paper 3 contains a single case study or investigation question (IQ). The question starts off with a scenario, which 'sets the scene' for the question. Students will be asked to use selected information in the three or so Extracts in the question, and also their general knowledge, to write answers written in the style of an economist providing advice to a client. The client could be, among others, a government department, a local authority, a regulatory body, a trade body or a trade union. Because the investigation in Part B of Paper 3 follows the 30 MCQs in Part A, the three sub-parts of the question are numbered [31], [32] and [33]. The maximum marks for the three sub-parts to the question will be [31]: 10 marks; [32]: 15 marks and [33]: 25 marks.

Students reading this guide could use the questions for revision purposes. All the questions can be used 'en bloc' as part of a short trial or mock exam near the end of your course. Alternatively, as you study a topic in the Content Guidance section of the guide, you could refer selectively to particular questions in this section that assess aspects of the topic.

This section of the Study Guide also contains:

- correct answers for the MCQs
- comments on the MCQs, explaining particular features of each question
- a student answer to each of the DRQs and for the investigation question
- comments on each student's answer explaining, where relevant, how the answer could be improved even though, as it stands, it is already a grade A* (or A) standard answer. These comments are denoted by the icon ⓔ.

■ Multiple-choice questions

Note: The 15 multiple-choice questions that follow provide examples of questions set in Part A of Paper 3 in the A-level examination. Each question is followed by a short guidance note prefaced with the icon ⓔ. The correct answers, along with brief explanatory notes explaining the correct answer and any other matter relevant to avoiding choosing a wrong answer (known as a distracter), follow on from the questions.

Question 1 The objectives of government economic policy

Which of the following is *not* a major objective of government economic policy in the UK?

A   Low unemployment.

B   Control of inflation.

C   A satisfactory and sustainable rate of economic growth.

D   The use of Bank Rate in monetary policy.

ⓔ This question is inviting you to confuse policy objectives with policy instruments.

Question 2 Interpretation of index numbers

The table below shows real gross domestic product (GDP) for an economy, expressed as index numbers.

Year	GDP (2015 = 100)
2013	90
2014	96
2015	100
2016	105
2017	112

Between 2013 and 2017, there must have been an increase in:

A   Aggregate demand.

B   The size of the working population.

C   The price level.

D   The government's budget surplus.

ⓔ You should expect one question on either the interpretation of, or the calculation of, index numbers in the multiple-choice section of the Paper 3 examination.

Question 3 Interpreting national income information

The table below shows the actual rate of growth in real national income in Country Z over 5 successive years.

Year	Percentage rate of growth in real income
2014	2.1%
2015	1.8%
2016	0.3%
2017	0.1%
2018	2.1%

Between 2014 and 2018:

A Nominal national income must have fallen.

B Country Z's trend rate of growth was zero.

C Aggregate demand increased.

D The economy entered recession.

ⓔ Make sure you understand the difference between levels and changes in levels.

Question 4 Investment

When an increase in national income leads to a change in investment, this illustrates the:

A Marginal propensity to consume.

B Accelerator.

C Boom phase of the economic cycle.

D Short-run economic growth.

ⓔ This question is testing your understanding of key macroeconomic concepts.

Question 5 The effect of a change in the size of the marginal propensity to consume on economic activity

If the size of the marginal propensity to consume is 0.4 and government spending increases by £10 billion:

A There will be an accelerator effect which stimulates the economy.

B National income will increase by approximately £16.7 billion.

C The size of the multiplier will fall.

D Expansionary monetary policy is operating.

ⓔ Make sure you can perform a simple multiplier calculation.

Question 6 Aggregate demand and supply

The following diagram shows an aggregate demand curve, a short-run aggregate supply curve and a long-run aggregate supply curve.

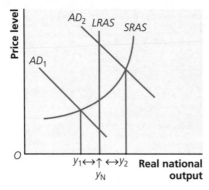

With respect to the diagram, all the following statements are true *except* one. Which statement is *untrue*?

A At y_2, there is a positive output gap.

B Given the position of the *LRAS* curve, it is impossible to produce output y_2.

C An increase in aggregate demand increases both real output and the price level.

D At y_1, there is a negative output gap.

e Make sure you understand the meaning of both positive and negative output gaps.

Question 7 Economic growth

The diagram below shows economic growth taking place in an economy.

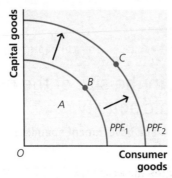

The movement from point *A* to point *C* shows:

A First short-run and then long-run growth taking place.

B Only long-run growth taking place.

C Negative economic growth taking place.

D Only short-run growth taking place.

ⓔ This question is testing your knowledge and understanding of short-run and long-run economic growth.

Question 8 The economic cycle

The various phases of the economic cycle show changes in:

A   Trend output.

B   The rate of inflation.

C   Actual output.

D   Seasonal unemployment.

ⓔ Make sure you don't confuse levels of actual output and trend output with changes in the rate of growth of actual and trend output.

Question 9 The natural rate of unemployment, inflation and the Phillips curve

The following diagram shows two short-run Phillips curves and the long-run Phillips curve.

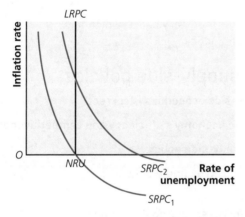

If the government increases aggregate demand to reduce unemployment below its natural rate (NRU):

A   The inflation rate falls below zero.

B   The long-run Phillips curve shifts leftwards.

C   A trade-off takes place along the long-run Phillips curve *LRPC*.

D   The inflation rate increases.

ⓔ Make sure you don't confuse a short-run Phillips curve with an *AD* curve.

Question 10 Financial markets

A main function of a capital market is to provide:

A   Liquidity to the banking system.

B   Capital goods to firms undertaking investment.

C   Foreign exchange to finance trade between countries.

D   Long-term finance to public limited companies (PLCs).

ⓔ Expect multiple-choice questions on the main types of financial markets.

Question 11 Monetary policy

In the UK, conventional monetary policy involves the use of:

A   Quantitative easing.

B   Forward guidance.

C   Tax changes.

D   Changes in Bank Rate.

ⓔ Make sure you don't confuse the instruments of monetary policy, which this question is testing, with the objectives of monetary policy.

Question 12 Fiscal policy and supply-side policies

Which of the following statements about supply-side economics is correct?

A   Supply-side policies are used to improve the economy's efficiency and competitiveness.

B   Fiscal policy cannot be used as a part of supply-side policy.

C   Government spending on training schemes is an example of non-interventionist supply-side policy.

D   The main aim of supply-side policies is to increase aggregate demand.

ⓔ Remember that supply-side fiscal policy is probably the most important of all the supply-side policies.

Question 13 Trade and globalisation

Which of the following statements about trade and globalisation is correct?

A   Free trade has led to de-globalisation rather than to globalisation.

B   The creation of customs unions has had no effect on globalisation.

C   The imposition of tariffs has speeded up the globalisation process.

D   Trade liberalisation has contributed to globalisation.

ⓔ Many factors other than trade have led to globalisation.

Question 14 The balance of payments and exchange rates

The government of a country that has a persistent current account surplus
revalues its currency to reduce the surplus. This is an example of:

A   An expenditure-reducing policy.

B   Fiscal policy.

C   Supply-side policy.

D   An expenditure-switching policy.

ⓔ Questions on current account surpluses are rarer than those on current account deficits,
but you must still prepare for them.

Question 15 Economic development

The following graph shows the production possibility frontier of a particular country.

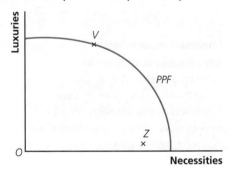

The movement from producing at point *Z* to point *V* represents:

A   Potential growth and development.

B   Actual growth but less development.

C   Actual growth and development.

D   Long-term growth and short-term development.

ⓔ Production possibility frontier diagrams are often used in MCQs to test your
knowledge of growth and development.

Answers to multiple-choice questions

Question 1	D	Question 6	B	Question 11	D
Question 2	A	Question 7	A	Question 12	A
Question 3	C	Question 8	C	Question 13	D
Question 4	B	Question 9	D	Question 14	D
Question 5	B	Question 10	D	Question 15	B

Comments on correct answers to MCQs

Question 1

Statements **A**, **B** and **C** list three of the standard objectives of macroeconomic policy and therefore don't provide the correct answer. Statement **D**, which states an instrument rather than an objective of macroeconomic policy, provides the correct answer.

Question 2

The fact that the size of the index numbers for real GDP shown in the table increased throughout the data period tells us that real GDP likewise increased. For the extra output to be purchased, aggregate demand must increase. This means that Statement **A** is the correct answer. None of the other statements can be deduced from the data.

Question 3

Although there is a slight possibility that nominal national income fell — if the price level fell by more than the increase in real national output — the word 'must' in Statement **A** makes this a wrong answer. Statement **B** is also wrong. The trend rate of growth cannot be calculated from just 5 years of data. Statement **D** is wrong because rising real output means that the economy can't be in recession. This leaves Statement **C** as the correct answer: as stated in the comment on MCQ 2, for the extra output to be purchased, aggregate demand must increase.

Question 4

When an increase in national income leads to a change in investment, this illustrates the accelerator. Statement **B** is therefore the correct answer. Statements **A**, **C** and **D** have no relevance to the question.

Question 5

Given that the marginal propensity to consume is 0.4, the marginal propensity to save is 0.6. This means that the size of the multiplier is 1/0.6, which is approximately 1.67. This in turn means that if government spending increases by £10 billion, national income increases by £10 billion x approximately 1.67, which is by approximately £16.7 billion. Statement **B** therefore provides the correct answer. None of the other statements can be deduced from the data.

Question 6

All the statements are true except Statement **B**, which provides the correct answer. In the short run, though not in the long run, it is possible to produce a level of output which is greater than the normal capacity level of output (y_N). Both Statements **A** and **D** are true with respect to positive and negative output gaps. Statement **C** is true because the initial macroeconomic equilibrium is to the left of the *LRAS* curve.

Question 7

An outward movement from a point *inside* a production possibility frontier to a point *on* the frontier depicts short-run economic growth, e.g. the movement from point *A* to point *B*. A movement from point *B* to a point on a further-out frontier shows long-run economic growth. Statement **A** states both events, so provides the correct answer. Statements **B** and **D** show only one type of growth, so both are wrong. Statement **C** is wrong because it is about negative economic growth rather than positive economic growth.

Question 8

Trend output is output adjusted to get rid of the fluctuations in actual output, so Statement **A** is incorrect. Changes in the rate of inflation may result from the fluctuations in the economic cycle, but the cycle shows changes in output rather than changes in the price level. This means that Statement **B** is wrong. Sometimes the cycle is measured in terms of changes in employment or unemployment, but not of changes in *seasonal* unemployment. Statement **D** is therefore wrong. This leaves Statement **C** as the correct answer — the phases of economic cycles are usually identified in terms of changes in actual output.

Question 9

The correct answer is provided by Statement **D**. An increase in aggregate demand, which is intended to reduce unemployment below its natural rate, will increase the rate of inflation. This means that Statement **A** is wrong. In the long run, the vertical *LRAS* curve shifts to the right, which means that Statement **B** is wrong. Statement **C** is wrong because trade-offs cannot take place along a vertical Phillips curve.

Question 10

The correct answer is Statement **D**. Statement **A** is wrong because money markets and not capital markets provide liquidity to the banking system. Statement **B** invites you to confuse providing capital goods such as machinery with the provision of long-term finance to PLCs, the latter mentioned in Statement **D** (the correct answer). Statement **C** is wrong because capital markets have little to do with foreign exchange markets and the financing of trade.

Question 11

Quantitative easing (QE) and forward guidance are two forms of *unconventional* monetary policy introduced during and after the 2008/09 recession precisely because *conventional* monetary policy (changing Bank Rate) was becoming ineffective as a method of stimulating aggregate demand. Hence, Statements **A** and **B** are wrong and Statement **D** is correct. Statement **C** is wrong because it is not about monetary policy.

Question 12

Statements **B**, **C** and **D** are all wrong. In the case of Statement **B**, fiscal policy is perhaps the most important part of supply-side policy, though other policies such as privatisation are also significant. With Statement **C**, government spending on training schemes is a part of interventionist rather than non-interventionist supply-side policy. Statement **D** is wrong because the 'main' aim of supply-side policies is to increase the economy's ability to *supply* more goods, though some increase in aggregate demand may be necessary to allow extra output to be sold. This leaves Statement **A** as the correct answer: the statement provides a good definition of supply-side policies.

Question 13

Statement **D** provides the correct answer: arguably trade liberalisation (reducing or eliminating import controls) is the most important facet of globalisation. Statement **A** invites you to confuse globalisation and de-globalisation, and similarly Statement **C** invites confusing the imposition of tariffs with their reduction or elimination. Finally, Statement **B** is incorrect because the creation of customs unions will have had *some* effect, for good or for bad, on globalisation.

Question 14

Statement **D** provides the correct answer. Statement **A** would be correct if the question were about correcting a current account deficit rather than a surplus, but in the context of the actual question, it is wrong. Revaluation is not an example of either fiscal policy or supply-side policy (though it could be an example of monetary policy), so Statements **B** and **C** are wrong. Statement **D** is correct because raising the exchange rate switches domestic spending away from imported goods and towards domestically produced goods.

Question 15

The correct answer is Statement **B**. The diagram shows that much of the increase in the output of luxury goods comes at the expense of necessities, the production of which falls. This is not an outcome consistent with economic development. However, short-run or 'actual' growth occurs, evidenced by the movement from a point *inside* the production possibility frontier (Z) to a point *on* the frontier (V). Statements **A**, **C** and **D** are either wrong or irrelevant.

■ Data-response questions

Note: The two data-response questions that follow provide examples of questions typical of those set in Part A of Paper 2 in the A-level examination. Each part of the questions is followed by a short guidance note, denoted by the icon ⊜. A student answer, along with comments (denoted by the icon ⊜), follows each question.

Context 1

Growth and macroeconomic performance

Read Extracts A, B and C, and then answer the questions that follow.

Extract A Average annual growth rates in the BRICs and in the USA, Japan and the UK, 2001 to 2014

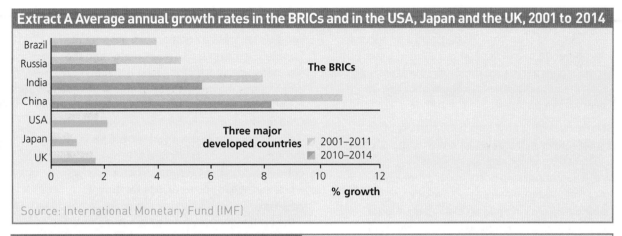

Source: International Monetary Fund (IMF)

Extract B Slowdown in the BRIC economies

In 2001 the Goldman Sachs economist Jim O'Neill coined the term 'BRIC countries' (Brazil, Russia, India and China) to describe the four most powerful emerging-market countries at a similar stage of economic development and all generally 5 experiencing a fast rate of economic growth. The term has come into general use as a symbol of the shift in global economic power away from already developed economies. It has been estimated that because of their sheer size and 10 high growth rates that have proved remarkably resistant to recession, China and India will overtake the seven largest developed economies by the end of the third decade of the twenty-first century. 15

The leading BRIC country, China, has experienced very high rates of economic growth — an average of 10% a year — since the 1990s. China's growth has been based on successful export growth and on a very high rate of investment — 48% of GDP. 20 However, many of China's investment projects have proved to be wasteful and unprofitable.

The Chinese government is trying to slow down growth and sell more consumer goods domestically. But it might be impossible to rein in 25 growth gradually without triggering widespread failure of ambitious investment projects.

Another one of the BRICs with clear problems is Brazil. Like Russia, it's an economy where commodity exports, in Brazil's case iron ore and 30 agricultural commodities, have played an important role in Brazil's success. To prevent itself falling deep into recession, Brazil needs to take steps to reduce its dependency on the export of commodities. It also needs to improve its labour competitiveness, 35 to make the country more attractive for private investment in other industries.

But early in 2016, Brazil is suffering a long and deep recession. By the end of 2016 Brazil's economy may be 8% smaller than it was in the first quarter 40 of 2014, when it last saw growth; GDP per person could be down by a fifth since its peak in 2010, which is not, according to *The Economist* magazine, as bad as the situation in Greece, but not far off.

Source: News reports, 2016

Extract C

It has been said that 'when America sneezes, the rest of the world catches a cold'. For example, when the USA suffers a recession, consumer and business confidence fall in other countries such as the UK, as do exports to, and foreign direct 5 investment (FDI) from, the United States.

However, emerging-market economies have been much less affected by recession and

economic slowdown in America and indeed in countries such as the UK. Some economists now 10 suggest that the UK should 'de-couple' from the US economy and align its economy much more closely with the BRIC countries and other emerging-market economies.

This is easier said than done. The influential 15 Ernst & Young Item Club recently noted that the →

UK has consistently lost share of global exports in recent years. The Item Club attributed this to a combination of a lack of penetration of emerging markets, in particular the BRIC countries, and a 20 loss of competitiveness brought about by an overvalued pound.

However, although it lags behind many of its competitors in the developed world, the UK has made some encouraging progress in 25 re-orientating its exports toward emerging markets. Also encouraging have been rising standards of living and an expanding middle class in the BRIC countries. The demands of these economies are becoming more closely 30

aligned to the goods and services in which the UK can demonstrate a comparative advantage. Competitiveness is also a key factor and the German experience of the past decade emphasises the importance of competitiveness 35 in helping to penetrate the BRIC markets. The Item Club thinks it unlikely the UK can replicate the German success in the short term. This is due to the need for stronger productivity growth which is only likely to occur through structural reform in 40 education and in encouraging investment. However, the UK should receive a significant boost if the exchange rate of the pound remains weak. This will support exports to the BRICs.

Source: News reports, 2016

[01] Using the data in Extract A, calculate the percentage change in China's annual growth rate between the periods 2001 to 2011 and 2010 to 2014. [2 marks]

ⓔ For each of the countries, the data show the average percentage rate of economic growth over two slightly overlapping periods. The question asks for a calculation, for China, of the percentage *change* in the growth rate when comparing the two sets of years.

[02] Explain how the data in Extract A show that the growth performance of the three developed countries improved from 2010 onward compared to the growth performance of the four BRIC countries. [4 marks]

ⓔ For each country, its average growth rate for a particular period of years is shown in two 'bars', one blue and one pink. Your answer should be based on the story told by these bars.

[03] Lines 18–20 of Extract B state that one of the causes of China's high rate of economic growth has been a high rate of investment. With the help of at least one diagram, explain the meaning of investment and how investment can lead to economic growth. [9 marks]

ⓔ Consider both the 'demand-side' and the 'supply-side' effects of investment. Make sure you include at least one diagram in your answer.

[04] 'Some economists now suggest that the UK should "de-couple" from the US economy and align its economy much more closely with the BRIC countries and other emerging-market economies.' (Extract C, lines 10–14)

Using the data and your economic knowledge, evaluate the possible impact on UK macroeconomic performance of de-coupling from the US economy and aligning the UK economy much more closely with the BRIC countries and other emerging-market economies. [25 marks]

ℯ The parts of AQA context, essay and investigation questions which ask for economic analysis and evaluation often include the words 'macroeconomic performance' or concepts such as 'macroeconomic stability'. If you see these words in a question, make sure you write a sentence or so explaining what you think they mean.

Student answer

[01] China's growth rate in 2001–11 was 10.8%; and in 2010–14 it was 8.1% (10.8 – 8.1 / 10.8) x 100 = –25%).

ℯ **2/2 marks awarded.** A correct calculation which earns full marks.

[02] For the years 2001–11, the data show that the four BRIC economies grew at a faster rate than in 2010–14. In each country growth was at least 2% higher in 2001–11 than in 2010–14. For example, India's growth was 7.8% in the first period compared to 5.3% in the second. In contrast, economic growth was faster in the three developed countries in 2010–14 than in 2001–11. Out of the three developed countries, the USA experienced the highest increase in growth, moving from 1.8% in 2001–11 to 2% in 2010–14.

ℯ **4/4 marks awarded.** An accurate answer that does enough to earn all 4 marks.

[03] Investment is when firms purchase capital goods to enhance production or when governments spend money on infrastructure projects to improve the capacity of the wider economy. Investment spending can improve economic growth in two main ways.

First, investment can lead to demand-side growth. Investment is a component of aggregate demand, which is defined with the formula $AD = C + I + G + (X - M)$. In the UK, investment accounts for approximately 18% of aggregate demand. Hence an increase in investment spending means that firms will be purchasing more capital goods and governments will be spending money on building projects. The increased demand for resources will shift the aggregate demand curve to the right, and increase the level of economic growth.

Second, investment spending will increase the capacity of the economy in the long run. Investment is the engine of long-term economic growth. If firms use investment spending to buy capital goods which enhances their productive capacity they will be able to increase production and reduce costs. This can be achieved either by expanding the scale of production so that the firm benefits from economies of scale and average costs fall, or by introducing more efficient technology which maximises outputs and cuts waste. Governments can also increase the capacity of the economy by spending on infrastructure projects such as high speed broadband or improved transportation networks that allow businesses and households to operate more efficiently in the wider economy.

Questions & Answers

ⓔ 5/9 marks awarded. The answer earns all the available 5 marks for the written part. Unfortunately, the student has disobeyed the instruction to include a diagram. This instruction is generally present in a part [03] or [07] question. Mark schemes will advise examiners that 'if the response does not include a relevant diagram, the student cannot be awarded more than 5 marks'. Only one diagram would be required, for example showing the effect of the *AD* curve shifting to the right. A second diagram might be a long-run rightward shift of the *LRAS* curve, or an outward movement of an economy's production possibility frontier.

[04] When evaluating the effect of de-coupling from the US economy and realigning with the BRIC economies, economists need to assess the impact on the UK's long-term economic growth, employment and balance of payments position. At present the UK conducts just under 50% of its trade with the EU, 15% with the USA and less than 10% with the BRIC countries. If the UK de-couples from the US (and the EU) it would require UK businesses to significantly re-orientate their patterns of trade and establish a strong presence in the emerging markets.

The strongest arguments for de-coupling are based on future economic growth. Economic power is shifting from the west to the east and the BRIC economies are going to be the dominant markets in the future. As Extract B states: 'China and India will overtake the seven largest developed economies by the end of the third decade of the twenty-first century'. Therefore, it makes sense for the UK to seek to trade with the economies that are experiencing strong growth. The data in Extract A show that even when it was slowing down in the years 2010–14, China's economy grew by 8%. In contrast, the US economy only grew by 2%, which was an improvement on its 1.8% growth rate in the years 2001–11.

If the UK can successfully align with the BRIC economies and sell exports to businesses and households experiencing strong income growth then it should result in a significant improvement to the UK's macroeconomic performance. Exports are a component of aggregate demand. If British firms can increase sales to the BRICs it will lead to export-led growth, which will increase real national output in the UK. China has a population of 1.3bn people, India 1.1bn and Brazil 200m, so potential export markets are very large. If British firms successfully sell more exports, then they will need to increase production and hire more workers, which should result in higher levels of employment and lower unemployment.

There are good opportunities for UK businesses to export products to the BRIC countries. Russia and Brazil are resource rich economies and have enjoyed strong growth from selling oil, gas, iron ore and agricultural products. China has built its growth on low-end manufacturing. Since 1990 the Chinese economy has created hundreds of millions of jobs and there is a growing Chinese middle class. The UK in contrast has a strong service sector economy and high-end manufacturing and fashion brands. UK firms could potentially enjoy significant success selling to

➜

the emerging middle classes in the BRIC countries but British business leaders have a lot of work to do. According to the Ernst & Young Item Club report in Extract C, the UK has 'consistently lost market share of global exports'. The report cites an overvalued pound and the lack of market penetration in the emerging markets.

The governing authorities could seek to make British exports more price competitive by devaluing sterling but this would hurt domestic households by increasing the cost of imports. The UK is dependent on importing food and energy. When the value of sterling depreciated against the dollar by 25% in 2009, British households experienced significant cost-push inflation and a fall in their purchasing power as the price of food and energy increased in supermarkets and on the forecourts of petrol stations. In the long run for sure, a better policy would be for the British government to focus on supply-side reforms. The Item Club report identifies the importance of 'productivity growth which is only likely to occur through structural reform in education and in encouraging investment'.

The extent to which the UK de-couples from the USA should be questioned. Although the British economy may suffer from a slowdown in the growth of the US economy, realigning with the BRICs will have its dangers. The BRIC countries are developing very quickly but they are prone to much greater swings of volatility in their economic cycles. Emerging economies do not have the automatic stabilisers that developed countries have. Western economies have progressive tax systems that cool consumer spending in a boom and social security payments that stabilise aggregate demand in a recession. Developing economies do not have these automatic stabilisers, which means that if they fall into deep recessions UK firms might find that their export sales will rapidly fall. At present the Brazilian economy is suffering from a deep recession and, according to Extract B, by the end of 2016 'its economy may be 8% smaller than it was in the first quarter of 2014'. At present Brazil is a minor export market for the UK, but if Britain does de-couple from the USA and realign it will be exposed to greater risks.

Ultimately the UK should seek to sell exports to the fast growing markets in the BRIC economies. Economic power is shifting to the east and British firms will enjoy significant success if they can take advantage of the opportunities that exist. If British firms can sell more high quality goods and services then it will result in strong export-led growth and increased employment for workers in these sectors. However, it does not necessarily follow that the UK has to break away from the USA. The USA will continue to be a large export market for British firms with high levels of household incomes and a similar language and culture. The USA may not grow as quickly as the emerging markets but it is a much more stable economy to trade with and British businesses have well-established trade links.

ⓔ **21/25 marks awarded.** This is a well-focused and well-written answer, which reaches Level 5 (21–25 marks). The answer displays a depth and breadth of relevant knowledge. The grade descriptor for a Level 5 answer is 'sound, focused analysis and well-supported evaluation'. On the critical side, the answer does not contain any diagrams to support the analysis. While providing an excellent overview, the answer is a bit thin on detailed analysis.

ⓔ Total score: 32/40 marks = Grade A*

Context 2

Government debt and deficits

Read Extracts D, E and F, and then answer the questions that follow.

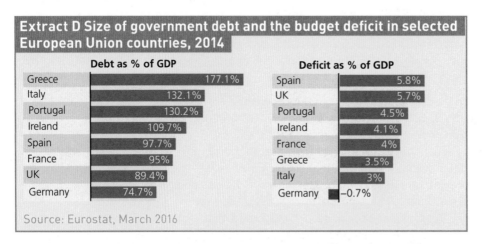

Extract D Size of government debt and the budget deficit in selected European Union countries, 2014

Debt as % of GDP		Deficit as % of GDP	
Greece	177.1%	Spain	5.8%
Italy	132.1%	UK	5.7%
Portugal	130.2%	Portugal	4.5%
Ireland	109.7%	Ireland	4.1%
Spain	97.7%	France	4%
France	95%	Greece	3.5%
UK	89.4%	Italy	3%
Germany	74.7%	Germany	−0.7%

Source: Eurostat, March 2016

Extract E Does government borrowing lead to economic problems?

For several decades, the UK government has generally run a budget deficit. The same has been true in many other developed economies, including the USA and in many of the countries that now form the eurozone. 5

Until recently, however, budget deficits and the borrowing that finances them were not seen by most economists to be a problem. There were two reasons for this. First, budget deficits functioned as an economic stabiliser, smoothing the volatility 10 of the fluctuations in the economic cycle and preventing recessions from becoming too deep.

Second, few people within the economy doubted the credit rating of government. Governments, or rather the 'ships of state', were regarded 'as safe 15 as houses' and more attractive to lend to than anyone else in the economy. This meant that governments could finance large budget deficits by borrowing primarily from the country's own citizens.

This is no longer the case. First, in the 2008/09 20 recession and in the generally 'flat' economy that existed shortly afterward, budget deficits grew enormously in size. Second, governments now borrow, not only from their own citizens, but also on international financial markets. 25 The international banks and other financial institutions which lend to finance budget deficits no longer necessarily trust the credit ratings of the governments to whom they lend. To lend even greater sums to governments, international 30 banks demand higher interest rate payments. Many fear that the cost of borrowing would force debtor governments to default on repaying their loans, with some governments effectively becoming bankrupt. 35

→

This led to the emergence of the sovereign debt problem. Sovereign debt is the accumulated borrowing of sovereign states, which has not yet been paid back to those who have lent to finance the state's activities. 40

Source: News sources, 2016

Extract F The sovereign debt problem and the eurozone

Most of the older developed economies in the global economy have suffered to a greater or lesser extent from the sovereign debt problem. Sovereign debt imposes a constraint on a government's fiscal policy and public spending 5 programme. Severely affected countries, such as Greece in the southern part of the eurozone, have been forced into severe public spending cuts to try to get the government's finances in order. The countries of the northern eurozone, 10 such as Germany and Sweden, have been little affected by the sovereign debt problem.

Outside the eurozone, the UK lies somewhere between these two extremes. Although public spending has been cut, the budget 15 deficit remains stubbornly high. However, unlike eurozone countries, the UK can allow the pound's exchange rate to fall to improve international competitiveness. And the UK's credit rating has remained higher than that 20 of most eurozone countries. The danger, however, is that the UK's macroeconomic performance could be severely hit by further poor performance in the eurozone and indeed by a complete collapse of the eurozone. 25

Source: News sources, 2016

[01] Using the data in Extract D, calculate the median value of debt as a percentage of GDP.   [2 marks]

ⓔ Make sure you don't confuse a median value with a mean value. Take account of the fact that eight countries are shown for both government debt and budget deficits in Extract D. This makes the calculation slightly more complicated than would have been the case if an odd number of countries were listed.

[02] Assuming that the nominal value of UK GDP was £1600 billion, using the data in Extract D compare the nominal sizes of the UK government debt and the UK budget deficit in 2014.   [4 marks]

ⓔ The data in Extract D show both debt and the deficits as percentages of GDP, which provides a measure of their 'real values'. The question requires you to find their 'nominal' or 'money' values and then to compare the two numbers you arrive at.

[03] Explain how, by acting as an automatic stabiliser, a budget deficit helps in the macroeconomic management of the economy.   [9 marks]

ⓔ To address this question fully, you should explain what is meant by an automatic stabiliser, before going on to the macroeconomic management of the economy.

[04] Using the data and your knowledge of recent economic events, evaluate the effect on UK macroeconomic performance of large budget deficits recently run both in the UK and in eurozone economies.   [25 marks]

ⓔ AQA defines 'recent events' in terms of about 15 years before the exam you sit. However, it would probably be wise to stick to the years since the beginning of the 'great recession' in 2008.

Questions & Answers

Student answer

[01] (109.7 + 97.7) / 2. The data in Extract D are arranged in descending order of the value of debt as a percent of GDP. This means that the median value is going to be the number half way down the list of eight numbers. However, because there are eight numbers in the list, I have taken the two middle numbers (109.7% and 97.7%), added them together, and divided by two. Thus my answer is 103.7%.

e 2/2 marks awarded. A correct calculation, which earns full marks. The student has correctly explained how they made their calculation. This means that if the student had made a slip in the calculation, they would have earned 1 of the 2 available marks. Don't, however, spend too much time showing how you have made your calculation.

[02] The UK national debt was 89.4% of £1,600 billion, which is £1,430.4 billion. The UK budget deficit was 5.7% of £1,600 billion, which is £91.2 billion.

e 2/4 marks awarded. Although the student has made a correct calculation, they have not compared the two figures they arrive at. The comparison would focus on the fact that the budget deficit as a % of GDP is much smaller than the national debt as a % of GDP. (The explanation for this, which is not required by the question, stems from the fact that the deficit is measured for just 1 year, whereas the national debt, being an economic stock, is a historical accumulation over many years, which leads to a much bigger number.)

[03] A budget deficit is when a government needs to borrow money to pay for its spending plans because there is a shortfall in taxation revenue. Budget deficits are an economic flow and are measured annually. A budget deficit will contribute to the national debt, which is the historical accumulation of all unpaid budget deficits.

A budget deficit can act as an automatic stabiliser to the economy during a recession in two main ways. First, by running a budget deficit the government is able to increase spending on social security payments for unemployed workers laid off by firms in a downturn. In a recession households will reduce spending and the demand for goods and services will fall. Consumption spending will fall and the level of aggregate demand will in turn fall. In response businesses will cut back on production and the demand for labour will fall. As a result the level of unemployment will rise, and the government's fiscal position will worsen as the number of claimants seeking welfare increases and income tax revenues fall. By running a budget deficit the government can increase spending on welfare, which ensures that unemployed households are guaranteed a minimum income. Workless households will use welfare payments to buy essential goods and services, which will prevent consumer spending from declining too sharply, which should act as an automatic stabiliser.

Second, the government can use the budget deficit to cut taxes to stimulate consumer spending and help businesses. In November 2008, the →

Labour government cut VAT from 17.5% to 15% as a temporary measure to stabilise the UK economy following the onset of the Great Recession. The aim was to help businesses cut costs and lower prices so that they could encourage households to maintain spending in the face of a deep recession. The temporary cut in VAT increased the UK's budget deficit by £10bn, which helped to stabilise aggregate demand.

ⓔ **4/9 marks awarded.** Although the answer attempts to answer the set question, overall it reaches the bottom of Level 2 in the mark scheme (4–6 marks) but not the higher Level 3 (7–9 marks). The first reason for this is the lack of a precise definition of a budget deficit in the first paragraph (it is defined in terms of government borrowing rather than as the difference between government spending and revenue). However, a rather more significant reason for this being a Level 2 rather than a Level 3 answer relates to the fact that the student does not fully understand how automatic stabilisers operate. The student argues that government decisions to change public spending and tax rates explains automatic stabilisers. This is wrong. The word 'automatic' in the term means that if the economy moves into recession, the size of the budget deficit *automatically* increases because tax revenues *automatically* fall and spending on unemployment benefits *automatically* goes up. Discretionary changes to tax rates and public spending are not involved. See the Content Guidance section of this guide to remind yourself of the meaning of an automatic stabiliser.

[04] The UK's macroeconomic performance can be evaluated by examining how high budget deficits have affected economic growth, the level of employment and the rate of inflation in recent years. Since the Great Recession in 2008, the British and eurozone governments have run exceptionally high budget deficits by the standards of previous years. The resulting level of borrowing has resulted in governments significantly increasing their national debts. Within the EU, this has led to two eurozone crises and to major doubts about the future of the eurozone itself.

In the immediate aftermath of the Great Recession the large budget deficits were necessary to prevent the complete collapse of the North Atlantic economic system. If the British and European governments had not run large budget deficits then they would not have been able to bail out the banking system or maintain welfare spending in response to mass unemployment. As Extract E says: 'budget deficits functioned as an economic stabiliser' and this prevented the recession from 'becoming too deep'. Had the British government not rescued the banks in October 2008 it is likely that the British economy would have completely broken down. RBS and HBOS were two of the biggest banks in the world and if they had not been rescued it is likely that other banks would have failed and the entire financial system would have stopped working. This would have been disastrous and the UK economy would have shrunk by more than 7% of GDP. Unemployment would have risen by more than 3m, instead of 2.8m. Deflation would have become a major problem rather than the temporary phenomenon of 2009. →

However, in the longer term the large budget deficits are causing problems for the UK's macroeconomic performance. The continued high levels of government borrowing have raised serious questions about many governments' ability to repay their debts in the future. As the data in Extract D illustrate, the eurozone countries Greece, Italy, Portugal, Ireland and Spain have exceptionally high levels of national debt and continue to run very large budget deficits. Greece, for example, has a national debt which is 177.1% of GDP and ran a budget deficit in 2014 that was 3.5% of GDP. Governments find it difficult to borrow money on the bond markets if they cannot explain how they plan to realistically run budget surpluses in the future. As Extract E explains, if the financial markets do not 'trust' a government they will demand a higher rate of interest when they lend to it in order to offset the risks of a sovereign debt default. However, this has so far led to two eurozone crises and the weaker eurozone countries asking the German government for a bailout to continue to avoid defaulting on debt repayments.

This situation has had major negative effects on the UK's macroeconomic performance. The UK has been affected by the economic uncertainty caused by the eurozone crises. Household and business confidence across the eurozone has been seriously harmed by the fears the eurozone may either expel countries such as Greece or break up. As a result, British firms that export to the eurozone have found that demand for their products has been disappointing. Exports are a component of aggregate demand. The UK sells around 50% of its exports to the European Union so this has had a significant effect on the UK's economic growth. This problem has been exacerbated by the austerity policies that the European Commission and German government have insisted on as part of the bailout packages given to Greece, Spain and Portugal. Deep cuts in welfare and increases in taxation have hit eurozone households hard and demand for British exports has been disappointing.

Like the weaker eurozone countries, the UK has continued to run large budget deficits. In 2009 the UK's budget deficit was over 14% of GDP and as Extract D shows in 2014 it was still the second highest in the countries shown at 5.7% of GDP. Unlike some of the eurozone countries Britain has not found it difficult to continue to borrow from the financial markets. This is partly because its national debt is still relatively low at 89.4% of GDP (Extract D) when compared to other European countries. It is also because the British government has maintained the general support of the credit rating agencies that it will be able to run budget surpluses in the foreseeable future. As a result the UK has been able to engage in fiscal easing and continue to run budget deficits. This has enabled the chancellor of the exchequer to delay tax increases, such as those planned on fuel duty, and slow the pace of budget cuts. Osborne initially planned to eliminate the deficit on current spending by 2015 but this has now been put back to 2020. As a result the British economy has been able to enjoy relatively higher economic growth and falling unemployment when compared to other European countries.

→

While governments can run large budget deficits in the short run they need to maintain the confidence of the markets in the long run. A government that does not have a credible fiscal policy will not be trusted by the financial markets and will struggle to borrow to finance its expenditure. The eurozone crises brought on by the high levels of sovereign debt have shaken the economies of the UK's main export markets. This has affected the British economy and undermined the household and business confidence of the continent. The UK government has sought to implement a major deficit reduction programme since 2010 but in the face of economic stagnation tax rises and spending cuts have been eased. This has enabled the UK economy to enjoy some of the highest levels of growth and lowest levels of unemployment in the European Union.

e **20/25 marks awarded.** To emphasise once again, when answering the final part of a data-response question or the second part of an essay question, to earn a high mark you have to evaluate as well as analyse. The analysis in this answer is accurate and well presented, and there is reasonable evaluation, but the answer lacks a 'rounding off' conclusion. Partly for this reason, we have placed the answer at the top of Level 4 (16–20 marks) for which the descriptor is 'sound, focused analysis and some supported evaluation'.

e Total score: 28/40 marks = high Grade A

■ Essay questions

Note: The three essay questions that follow provide examples of questions typical of those set in Part B of Paper 2 in the A-level examination. Each part of the questions is followed by a short guidance note, denoted by the icon *e*. A student answer, along with comments (denoted by the icon *e*), follows each question.

Essay 1 Unemployment

Total for this essay: 40 marks

[09] Carefully explain the meaning of the natural rate of unemployment. [15 marks]

e Make sure you don't confuse the *natural* rate of unemployment with the *normal* rate of unemployment, i.e. the rate of unemployment in a typical year.

[10] Evaluate the view that reducing the natural rate of unemployment is better for the economy than reducing unemployment below its natural rate. [25 marks]

e Students often confuse the two ideas mentioned in the question. Make sure you avoid this trap.

Student answer

[09] Monetarists and other free-market economists use the term 'the natural level of employment' to describe the level of employment at which the labour market clears — at the real wage rate at which the aggregate →

demand for labour equals the aggregate supply of labour. They argue that there is no involuntary unemployment when employment is at its natural level. However, there will be some voluntary frictional unemployment, which they call 'the natural level of unemployment'. (The natural rate of unemployment (NRU) is the natural level of unemployment calculated as a percentage of the labour force.)

The natural rate of unemployment can also be explained in terms of the long-run Phillips curve. In 1968, Milton Friedman introduced the theory of the expectations-augmented Phillips curve when he argued that a stable relationship between inflation and unemployment, as depicted by the original Phillips curve, had never existed. According to Friedman, the apparent relationship identified by Phillips was at best short term and unstable. Friedman's theory suggests that the only 'true' long-term relationship between unemployment and inflation lies along a vertical line, on which trade-offs are not possible, running through the natural rate of unemployment. This is the long-run Phillips curve (*LRPC*).

The relationship between the *LRPC* and the economy's aggregate labour market is shown in the diagram below. The economy's natural level of employment is determined in the upper panel of the diagram at the market-clearing real wage at which the aggregate demand for labour equals the aggregate supply of labour. The natural level of unemployment is then calculated by subtracting the natural level of employment from the total labour force. The diagram has been drawn so that the natural level of unemployment is depicted immediately below the natural level of employment in the upper panel. If either or both of the aggregate demand for, and aggregate supply of, labour curves shift rightwards in the upper panel, the natural level of employment will increase. Simultaneously, the *LRPC* and the natural level of unemployment will shift leftwards in the lower panel.

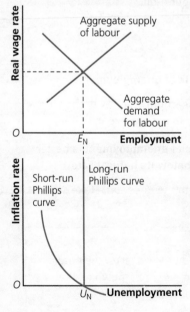

ⓔ **15/15 marks awarded.** This answer earns full marks. The student understands the NRU fully and has drawn excellent diagrams to support their answer.

[10] Free-market economists have sometimes argued that it is irresponsible to use Keynesian demand management policies to try to reduce unemployment below its natural rate. They argue that any (temporary) reduction of unemployment below its natural rate cannot be sustained. They believe that when demand expands to reduce unemployment below its natural rate, inflation always accelerates, and that accelerating inflation destroys the conditions in which a high level of employment can be maintained.

Most free-market economists want to reduce unemployment (though some argue that some unemployment is necessary to 'discipline' the workforce). They believe the correct way to reduce unemployment is to reduce the natural rate itself. Supply-side policies should be used for this purpose. But unlike the Keynesians, who in the past have recommended interventionist supply-side policies which increase the role of the government, free-market supply-side policy reduces the role of the state in the economy. Appropriate policies (for a free-market economist) include tax and public expenditure cuts to reduce the burden of taxation on the private sector and to create incentives to individuals and firms, and all microeconomic policies which might make individual markets more competitive, efficient and adaptable to change. Reductions in unemployment benefits are sometimes recommended, to reduce their value relative to take-home pay in a low-paid job.

Because free-market economists believe that it is irresponsible to expand demand to reduce unemployment below its natural rate, it is sometimes said that they reject demand expansion completely. For the most part, this is untrue, though some free-marketeers, the new-classical economists, believe that as output and employment are always at or very near their natural levels and rates, expansionary fiscal and monetary policy should only be used with very great caution. However, many free-market economists agree with the Keynesians that as long as unemployment is significantly above its natural rate (and output below its natural level), there is a role for demand expansion, primarily through lower interest rates and monetary policy. This will close the economy's negative output gap — the gap between actual output and the level of output that would occur had the economy been growing continuously at its trend rate of growth. They accept that temporary demand-deficient unemployment, in the form of cyclical unemployment, can exist in the recessionary phase of the business cycle, and that a demand stimulus is the appropriate response.

e **24/25 marks awarded.** This is a very good answer which contains a significant amount of accurate analysis and thoughtful evaluation. Quite rightly, the student accepts that virtually all economists, except extreme free-marketeers, now agree that demand management policies should be used to stabilise the economic cycle and to make sure that there is sufficient demand to absorb extra output produced by successful supply-side policies. The fact that most economists once again accept a role for demand management means that there is now an area of consensus and synthesis which unites rather than separates a large part of the economics profession.

e Total score: 39/40 marks = Grade A*

Essay 2 Monetary policy and fiscal policy

Total for this context: 40 marks

[11] **Distinguish between monetary and fiscal policy and explain how both can be used to manage aggregate demand.**
[15 marks]

e Along with supply-side policies, monetary policy and fiscal policy are the two examples of government macroeconomic policy you need to understand in some detail.

[12] **Evaluate the fiscal policy that might be implemented by a free-market-orientated government in the UK.**
[25 marks]

e To answer this question properly, you must understand the difference between demand-side fiscal policy and supply-side fiscal policy.

> **Student answer**
>
> **[11]** Monetary policy is the part of macroeconomic policy through which the government and also its central bank tries to achieve one or more of its policy objectives, by using monetary instruments such as controls on bank lending and the raising or lowering of interest rates. Likewise, fiscal policy is the part of government policy which uses fiscal instruments (altering the structure and rates of taxation, public spending and the public sector's budgetary position) to try to achieve the government's policy objectives.
>
> Fiscal policy and monetary policy may be assigned to different policy objectives; alternatively, they may be used to support each other or even to achieve the same objective, such as the management of aggregate demand. In the Keynesian era, fiscal policy was indeed associated primarily with the management of aggregate demand. However, since the Keynesian era ended in the 1970s, free-market-inspired governments have generally rejected the use of taxation and public spending as discretionary instruments of demand management. (The one exception occurred between 2008 and 2010 when the then UK Labour government revived Keynesian policies and implemented the so-called 'fiscal →

stimulus' to try to 'spend the economy out of recession'.) The election of the Conservative-dominated coalition government in 2010 brought the Keynesian fiscal stimulus to an end. The Conservative chancellor of the exchequer believes that when fiscal policy is used to stimulate or reflate aggregate demand in order to achieve economic growth and full employment, the policy will be at best ineffective, and at worst damaging. Any growth of output and employment will be short-lived, and in the long term the main effect is to accelerate inflation, thereby destroying the conditions necessary for satisfactory market performance and 'wealth creation'.

Both fiscal policy and monetary policy attempt to manage aggregate demand by shifting the aggregate demand (AD) curve rightward or leftward. The diagram below shows a rightward shift of aggregate demand, which increases real output from y_1 to y_2, and increases the price level in a demand-pull inflation from P_1 to P_2. Extra spending injected into the economy increases people's income. At the next stage, people spend a fraction of their increased income on consumption, which creates more income for other people. Multiple and successive stages of income generation follow, each smaller than the previous stage because a fraction of income received is held back and not spent.

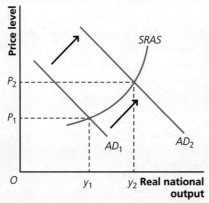

@ **11/15 marks awarded.** There is a danger of answering this question much too narrowly, namely by defining monetary policy solely in terms of 'monetarism' and fiscal policy in terms of 'Keynesian demand management'. Fortunately, this student does not do this. She writes a good answer, but nevertheless does not earn full marks. The student asserts that fiscal and monetary policy both shift the AD curve, but she needs to explain this. For example, she should explain how, in monetary policy, an interest rate cut stimulates consumption and investment.

[12] A free-market-orientated government would probably subordinate fiscal policy to the needs of monetary policy. Free-market economists believe that control of public spending and public sector borrowing (in the government's fiscal policy) is a necessary precondition for responsible control of monetary conditions in the economy (in monetary policy). Instead of using fiscal policy to manage demand, a free-market-orientated government might base policy on

→

a fiscal 'rule' to reduce public spending, taxation and government borrowing as proportions of national output. Besides reducing the inflationary effects of 'big government spending', such a fiscal policy should prevent public spending from 'crowding out' the private sector. Free-market economists believe that public sector spending and borrowing 'crowd out' the private sector in two ways. 'Resource crowding out' occurs when the government uses resources in its public spending programme which might otherwise have been employed in private sector production. Second, 'financial crowding out' occurs when the government borrows to finance public sector spending. An increase in government borrowing causes interest rates to rise, which increases the cost of investment finance for the private sector.

As well as adopting a fiscal policy which is consistent with the monetary policy aim of controlling inflation, free-market economists recommend that the macroeconomic elements of fiscal policy should be subordinated to a more microeconomic fiscal policy based on tax cuts to create incentives to work, save and be entrepreneurial. They argue that workers respond to cuts in income tax rates by working harder. Conversely, high rates of income tax and a high overall tax burden create disincentives which, by reducing national income as taxation increases, also reduce the government's total tax revenue.

Free-market economists argue that the increase in the tax burden in the Keynesian era, which was required to finance a growing government sector, raised the average tax rate towards or beyond the critical point at which tax revenue is maximised. In this situation, any further tax increases would have the perverse effect of reducing the government's total tax revenue still further. Indeed, tax cuts rather than tax increases may raise total tax revenue, since a growing national output, stimulated by lower tax rates, will yield higher total revenue despite the reduced tax rates. The effect is reinforced by a decline in tax evasion and avoidance as these activities become less worthwhile at less penal tax rates.

Given that governments have to levy taxes to raise revenue to finance necessary government expenditure, free-market economists believe that the structure or pattern of taxation should be switched away from taxes on income and capital and towards taxation on expenditure. All taxes are of course unpopular and disliked and resisted to some extent by taxpayers, but some are more unpopular than others. Free-market economists believe that expenditure taxes are less unpopular than income tax, and therefore more acceptable to taxpayers. Although initially disliked when first imposed or when tax rates are raised, expenditure taxes are less 'visible' than income taxes. Taxpayers soon get used to expenditure taxes and learn to live with them. Free-market economists also argue that expenditure taxes have a further significant advantage. Unlike income taxes, expenditure taxes do not have a substitution effect, which distorts the choice between labour and leisure — a distortion which supply-siders believe operates against the supply of labour and in favour of not working. Indeed, in so far as expenditure taxes — like all taxes — introduce some distortion into the

→

> economic system, they do so by raising the prices of consumer goods, which encourages households to substitute saving in place of consumption. This is an important virtue in the free-market view of the world.

(e) **23/25 marks awarded.** Students sometimes argue that because free-market economists generally reject the use of fiscal policy to manage the level of aggregate demand, this means that they do not recommend any use of fiscal policy. This student clearly rejects this erroneous line of approach and writes an excellent Level 5 answer (21–25 marks), detailing a range of possible ways in which free-market economists might (and do) use fiscal policy. AQA's mark descriptor for Level 5 is: 'Sound, focused analysis and well-supported evaluation. The answer is well organised, showing sound knowledge and understanding of economic terminology, concepts and principles with few, if any, errors; the answer includes good application of relevant economic principles and, where appropriate, good use of data to support the response; the answer includes well-focused analysis with clear, logical chains of reasoning; and there is supported evaluation throughout the response and in a final conclusion.' To reach Level 5, most but not necessarily all of these descriptors have to be met. In this case, there is no conclusion to 'wind up' the answer, but overall the answer reaches Level 5.

(e) Total score: 34/40 marks = Grade A*

Essay 3 The benefits and costs of globalisation

Total for this context: 40 marks

[13] Explain the main features of globalisation. [15 marks]

(e) As always, when answering the first part of an essay question (or the second part of a Context question) you should start your answer by defining the key concept in the question — in this case, globalisation. At the very minimum, you should try to identify at least three key features and explain each in some detail. It is probably unwise to bring in too many features, if all you then do is write a single sentence for each.

[14] Evaluate the view that everybody must benefit from globalisation. [25 marks]

(e) The word 'must' is a key word in this question. When words such as 'must', 'always', 'solely' and 'inevitably' appear in the last part of an essay or Context data-response question, your answer will not score highly if it agrees or disagrees 100% with the central assertion in the question. It is always best in your answer to adopt an 'it all depends' approach.

Student answer

[13] Globalisation is the name given to the processes that integrate all or most of the world's economies, making countries increasingly dependent on each other. Globalisation has been made possible by improvements in information and communication technology (ICT), as well as by developments in more traditional forms of technology. These include massive improvements in passenger air flights and containerisation, ➔

which has greatly reduced the cost of shifting freight around the world. Examples of globalisation include service industries in the UK dealing with customers through call centres in India, and fashion companies designing their products in Europe, making them in South East Asia and finally selling most of them in North America.

Two of the main features of globalisation are:

(i) the growth of international trade and the reduction of trade barriers — a process encouraged by the World Trade Organization (WTO). Globalisation involves the liberalising or freeing up of world trade. As a result of successive rounds of tariff reduction started in the 1940s, import duties have fallen. This allows specialisation and trade to take place in accordance with the principle of comparative advantage, which in turn increases production and consumption possibilities for most of the different countries in the global economy

(ii) greater international mobility of capital and to some extent of labour. Globalisation enables the movement of capital from developed economies to poor economies. In theory it also leads to labour mobility in the opposite direction. However, immigration controls slow down the movement of labour from poor to rich countries. Nevertheless, in recent years illegal immigration into developed economies has occurred because rich countries have informally encouraged migrants to fill the relatively low-paid jobs rejected by their own citizens

In summary, some of the other features of globalisation are:

(i) a significant increase in the power of international capitalism and multinational corporations (MNCs) or transnational companies

(ii) the deindustrialisation of older industrial regions and countries, and the movement of manufacturing industries to newly industrialised countries (NICs)

(iii) more recently, the movement of internationally mobile service industries, such as call centres and accounts offices, to NICs

(iv) a decrease in governmental power to influence decisions made by MNCs to shift economic activity between countries

@ **13/15 marks awarded.** The student clearly understands what globalisation is, defines the concept, and explains two of the main features of the process. Having done this, he then lists four other characteristics of globalisation but without really explaining them. Overall, this answer falls just short of full marks, as in this case the mark scheme requires explanation of a third feature of globalisation.

[14] Free-market economists generally support globalisation and regard its growth as inevitable. They argue that the benefits of further global economic integration, which include the extension of political freedom and democracy as well as the economic benefits of more production and higher living standards, significantly exceed the disadvantages, such as

→

the destruction of local cultures. But opponents argue that globalisation is a respectable name for the growing exploitation of the poor, mostly in developing countries, by international capitalism and US economic and cultural imperialism.

For its critics, low-paid workers in sweatshops, farmers in the developing world being forced to grow genetically modified crops, the privatisation of state-owned industry to qualify for IMF and World Bank loans, and the growing dominance of US corporate culture and multinational companies symbolise what is wrong with globalisation. According to this view, which I hold myself, globalisation has led to a 'McDonaldisation' or 'Coca-Colonisation' of significant parts of the world's economy. This has involved and continues to involve the destruction of local and national products, identities and cultures by US 'world brands'. The opposite process of 'glocalisation', or local action, is needed to prevent or offset the damage done by globalisation to vulnerable local cultures. Supporters of globalisation counter by arguing that people in the rest of the world demand US products because they consider them superior to traditional local produce.

Another feature of globalisation that has been criticised is the alleged treatment of local labour by multinational corporations. Companies such as Nike have been accused of selling trainers and footballs in developed countries such as the UK at prices far above the cost of raw materials and the low wages paid to the labour making the goods in developing countries. But in response, the multinationals argue that the 'low wages' they pay far exceed the local wages paid by firms indigenous to the countries in which they manufacture. They believe this encourages local wages to rise. MNCs also claim to improve health and safety and other labour market conditions in the poor countries in which they operate.

But by threatening to close down factories and to move production to poor countries, it is argued that MNCs also reduce wages and living standards in developed countries. Whether this is true depends, of course, on the type of jobs that emerge in developed countries to replace those lost through deindustrialisation and globalisation. Are the new jobs created in the highly skilled service sector, or are they menial, low-paid, unskilled 'McJobs'?

In recent decades, globalisation has considerably reduced the power of national governments, certainly in smaller countries, to control multinational firms operating within their boundaries. National governments have also lost much of the freedom to undertake the economic policies of their choice with respect to managing domestic economies. Governments enjoy less freedom to introduce tariffs and other import controls. At the same time, capital flows into and out of currencies severely constrain a government's ability to implement an independent monetary policy, even when the country's exchange rate is freely floating.

ⓔ **19/25 marks awarded.** In many ways this is a very good answer. Indeed, at least some of the answer could have been included in the answer to part [13] to pick up the extra marks needed there for explanation. However, although containing lots of relevant knowledge and argument, the answer does not reach Level 5. This is because the student has not directly addressed key words in the question: 'must' and 'everybody'. Obviously, not everybody gains from globalisation. The answer needs to indicate who the winners and losers are from the globalisation process. There is some implicit debate of this issue, which enables the answer to reach Level 4. Winners and losers may vary, of course, depending on the state of the global economy and of individual nation states within the global economy.

ⓔ Total score: 32/40 marks = low Grade A*

▌Investigation question

Note: The investigation question that follows provides an example of questions typical of those set in Part B of Paper 3 in the A-level examination. Each part of the question is followed by a short guidance note, denoted by the icon ⓔ. A student answer, along with comments (denoted by the icon ⓔ), follows on from the questions.

Should there be a return to protectionism?

Source booklet

Extract A: The case for free trade

Extract B: History debunks the free trade myth

Extract C: World trade and UK trade: selected statistics

Extract D: Employment in the UK clothing industry, 2014

Extract A The case for free trade

The case for free trade, correctly understood, is as powerful as ever. It deserves much stronger support. The basic case is robust, and the economic record of the world's richest economies attests to it: free trade makes economies more 5 productive by forcing producers to innovate, specialise and compete. Over time, free trade gives the economy as a whole a substantial boost.

There are exceptions to the argument that openness to free trade promotes growth, mostly 10 concerning the need to shelter infant industries in developing economies. It's also true that more trade involves winners and losers, and that gains for the overall economy aren't much use to the people who lose their jobs because of cheap   15 imports. But you could say the same of people who lose their jobs because of automation. A case can be argued that, without resorting to protectionism, we need to help the workers harmed by trade. But not by imposing high tariffs (and coping with the 20 barriers raised by other countries in retaliation). Import controls would involve huge disruptions in the short term, for both suppliers and workers. Later would come the high long-term costs traditionally associated with trade barriers.   25

Source: News reports, 2016

Extract B History debunks the free trade myth

Free-market economists believe that international specialisation and complete free trade, undertaken in accordance with the principle of comparative advantage, benefits all the countries involved. 5

However, not all economists agree. The Korean economist Ha-Joon Chang has written that 'History debunks the free trade myth'. Ha-Joon Chang's view is that governments in already developed economies are fully in favour of free 10 trade — but only if their countries face little or no competition from developing economies. As soon as such competition emerges, the rich countries 'pull up the drawbridge', arguing

that protectionism is necessary to protect 15 themselves from the 'unfair' competition coming from cheap labour countries.

Rich countries also argue that they need protecting from countries in the much poorer developing world which steal their technology 20 and clone their products, partly by ignoring international patent laws and other aspects of intellectual copyright. However, transfers of technology can be an important mechanism for stimulating the development of the world's less 25 prosperous economies.

Source: News reports

Extract C World trade and UK trade in clothing and footwear: selected statistics

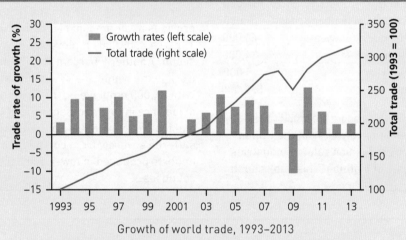

Growth of world trade, 1993–2013

Source: IMF, *World Economic Outlook*

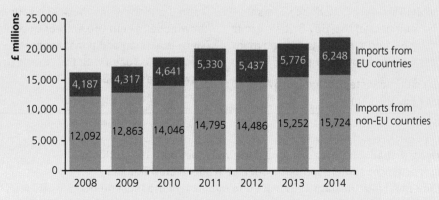

UK imports of finished clothing from EU and non-EU countries, 2008–2014

Source: World Trade Organization

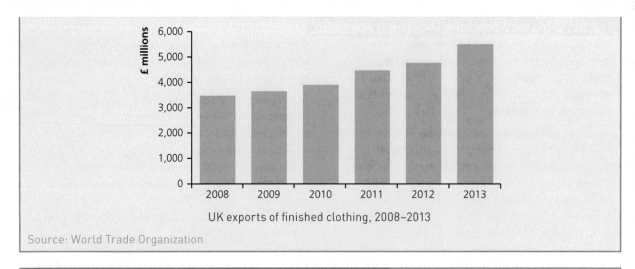

UK exports of finished clothing, 2008–2013

Source: World Trade Organization

Extract D Employment in the UK clothing industry, 2014

Employment in clothing-related industries:

Retail sale of clothing:	414,000
Retail sale of footwear and leather goods:	59,000
Wholesale of clothing and footwear:	43,000
Manufacture of clothing:	34,000
Manufacture of footwear:	5,000
Total employment:	**555,000**

Currently around 555,000 people are employed in fashion, textiles and fashion retail in the United Kingdom. Most jobs in fashion related industries are in the retail sale of clothing. This sub-industry employs 75 percent with 414,000 people working in the retail sale of clothing. Also the retail sale of footwear and leather goods provides a fair amount of jobs in fashion: about 11 percent, 59,000 employees, work within this sector. Another 8 percent, 43,000 employees, work in the wholesale of clothing and footwear. With 34,000 employees, the lowest number of jobs are in the manufacturing of clothing and footwear, an industrial sector which has suffered severely from competition from imports produced in low-wage developing countries.

Scenario

You are an economist reporting to a lobby group of UK clothing manufacturers called 'Buy British Clothing'. All the members of the 'Buy British' group have suffered falling sales in recent years and many former members have gone out of business.

The lobby group has requested that you provide answers to three key questions.

Referring to the source booklet, study Extracts A, B and C and then use these and your own economic knowledge to help you answer questions 31 and 32. There is also an additional news report, Extract D, which is to be used with the other extracts to help answer question 33.

[31] To what extent, if at all, do the data support the view that both UK clothing manufacturers and consumers benefit from free trade in clothing and footwear? You must use the data in Extract C to support your assessment. [10 marks]

ⓔ You must draw on the data to support the argument you make.

Student answer

[31] The data provide strong evidence that free trade has benefited UK
consumers and suppliers. Extract A sets out the theoretical economic
case, stating that 'free trade makes economies more productive by forcing
producers to innovate, specialise and compete'. Free trade means that
consumers have increased choice as they are able to purchase goods
at lower prices. As can be seen in the diagram below, when domestic
markets are opened up to international competition, consumers benefit
from lower prices.

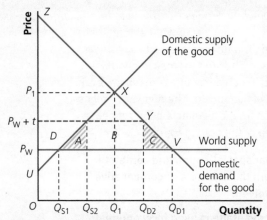

The diagram shows that as prices fall the consumer surplus increases.
Before the fall in price from $P_w + t$ to P_w, consumer surplus was the
triangular area bounded by the points $P_w + t$, Z and Y. After the fall in
price, the triangular area has increased in size by the 'wedge' bounded
by P_w, $P_w + t$, Y and V. The consumer surplus triangle indicates that most
households are willing to pay a high price for the product but are able to
buy the product at a lower price. Lower prices are good for consumers
because they are able to buy more goods and services with their
disposable incomes, which means that living standards increase.

The data in Extract C, Chart 2, show that between 2008 and 2014 the UK
imported more and more finished clothing. In this seven-year period
the value of imports increased by 49% from EU countries and 30% from
non-EU countries; although in most years, non-EU imports accounted for
roughly 70% of total imports.

Extract B suggests that UK clothing firms would be threatened by free
trade because of 'competition from cheap labour countries'. Given that
members of the Buy British group have suffered falling sales in recent
years, it is logical to assume that UK firms are struggling to export their
products.

However, the evidence suggests that UK clothing firms have benefited
from international trade in the same period. Chart 3 in Extract C shows
that in every year between 2008 and 2013 the value of UK exports of

→

> finished clothing increased. In 2008 the value of exports was £3,500m and by 2013 it had risen to £5,500m, an increase of 57%. This suggests that UK clothing firms have benefited from the long-term increases that have taken place in world and UK trade in clothing and footwear since 1993. In the 20 years between 1993 and 2013 trade grew in every year, except 2009, and total trade increased by 225%.
>
> Overall the data suggest that both UK consumers and producers have benefited from free trade since 2008.

e **10/10 marks awarded.** An excellent answer, which does exactly what is required by the wording of the question, namely to discuss to what extent, if at all, the data support the view that both UK clothing manufacturers and consumers benefit from free trade in clothing and footwear. The student makes good use of the data in Extract C and includes and explains an appropriate diagram, even though the question does not require the use of a diagram. The answer reaches the top of Level 3 (8–10 marks) in the mark scheme, providing a good response that is well organised and makes effective use of the data in Extract C.

[32] Lines 2–5 of Extract B state 'international specialisation and complete free trade, undertaken in accordance with the principle of comparative advantage, benefits all the countries involved.'

Explain how the theory of comparative advantage is used by economists to justify free trade and to oppose import controls and other forms of protectionism. [15 marks]

e This question requires explanation and analysis but not evaluation.

Student answer

[32] Comparative advantage is an economic model devised in the early nineteenth century by the classical economist David Ricardo that built upon the absolute advantage model of another classical economist, Adam Smith. Absolute advantage shows that if countries are better at producing a good than another country they should specialise in what they do best and then trade their surpluses. Comparative advantage is a more sophisticated model because it shows that as long as opportunity costs differ, countries can benefit from partial specialisation. Both trade models advocate free trade on the grounds that if countries specialise and trade then they can benefit from significant output gains. Economists assume that if countries are increasing the level of production then they are producing more consumer and capital goods. This will in turn lead to faster levels of economic growth and higher living standards. It is for this reason that Extract A favours free trade and resists protectionist trade barriers.

Trade barriers are introduced by a government with the aim of protecting domestic firms from cheaper international competition. As Extract B says, countries favour free trade when they 'face little or no competition' but once competition emerges they impose import controls to 'pull up the drawbridge'.

@ **8/15 marks awarded.** This answer is placed at the mid-point of Level 2 (6–10 marks) in the mark scheme, for which the descriptor includes: 'shows satisfactory knowledge and understanding of economic terminology, concepts and principles but some weaknesses may be present' and 'includes some reasonable analysis but which might not be adequately developed'. The main weakness in the answer is a lack of development and explanation of the meaning of comparative advantage. A sound numerical example would provide this development.

[33] Taking into account the information about the current state of employment in UK clothing industries outlined in Extract D, and the other evidence in the extracts, recommend and justify two courses of action that either the members of the lobby group or the government should undertake in order to make sure that British clothing manufacturers remain in business in future years. [25 marks]

@ The instruction to 'justify', means that you must evaluate the strength of the arguments you use in your answer.

Student answer

[33] Report to the members of Buy British Clothing Group

The clothing industry is highly competitive and in recent decades new competition from the emerging markets has put considerable pressure on British businesses. Between 1993 and 2013 world trade in the industry increased by 225% (Extract C, Chart 1), and in 2014 the UK imported 21,972m garments (Extract C, Chart 2). Britain has many successful brands but after having conducted an extensive investigation this report has put forward two main recommendations to the Buy British Clothing Group: first, to embrace free trade and global competition; and second British manufacturers must focus on the high quality top end of the market.

Option 1 Embrace free trade and global competition

While the European Commission has the power to introduce protectionist measures against imported clothing from low cost producers, this is a short-sighted approach for two reasons. First, as long as the UK remains in the EU, protectionism would lock UK firms into declining European markets and shut them off to the fast growing emerging markets. France, Italy and Spain may want to 'pull up the drawbridge' because they cannot compete with the 'unfair competition in the cheap labour countries' (Extract B), but this will lead to retaliation. If the EU introduces protection then it will become increasingly difficult for UK clothing firms to sell across the world because other countries will place tariffs on British exports.

Given that economic power is shifting to the East and the fastest levels of growth are coming from the BRIC economies, Buy British firms need to embrace global competition and not resist it. They need to try to sell their clothing to the billions of new consumers in India and China and not seek to protect their traditional domestic base. The European markets are ageing because demographically these societies are getting older. The emerging markets in the Far East in contrast are younger and levels of →

household income are predicted to rise in the future. Therefore, it would be foolish to seek to protect and look inward.

Second, by embracing free trade UK firms will become more competitive. Capitalism thrives on competition. As Extract A says 'free trade makes economies more productive by forcing producers to innovate, specialise and compete'. If British firms do not embrace free trade, with continued EU membership, they may find protectionist shelter in the EU but they will become less innovative and efficient. Over time their products will be seen to be second best and their prices too high. In the long run European and British consumers will demand the removal of trade restrictions so that they can buy the better made and better priced international clothing. International free trade gives consumers lower prices and raises domestic living standards. Producers may resist international competition but to resist it is not an option in the long run.

Option 2 Concentrate on the high end of the clothing market

The Buy British Clothing group needs to focus its manufacturing base on the high end of the clothing market. It is difficult to compete with the low end of the market, where there are thousands of overseas manufacturers making near identical products. This part of the market possesses many of the features of perfect competition. There are a large number of buyers and sellers, they cannot affect the ruling market price, there is very little product differentiation, barriers to entry are relatively low, and producers can sell in bulk without affecting the price. As a result the markets set the prices and firms are price-takers at price P_1, as shown in the diagram below:

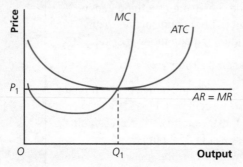

At this end of the market, firms located in emerging markets have a competitive advantage because they can employ cheap labour and still make normal profits by selling in large quantities. British firms have struggled to compete in this sector in recent decades and it is unwise to try to change this.

Finally, the majority of UK jobs in the clothing sector are in retail sales and not in manufacturing. The data in Extract D shows that 414,000 jobs are in the retail sales of clothing and a further 59,000 jobs in the retail sale of footwear and leather goods. This accounts for 75% of the employment in the UK clothing industry. Hence, if the Buy British Campaign wants to protect UK jobs, it must support the retail sector which imports millions of goods from non-EU and EU manufacturers every year.

→

The UK does have a vibrant manufacturing base in clothing but it is in the high quality sector of the market and is relatively small. Exports of finished clothing from the UK have grown every year since 2008 and in 2013 over £5,000m exports were sold (Extract C, Chart 3). This sector only accounts for 43,000 jobs (Extract D) but if it can continue to make high quality products then it may be very profitable. The key to this sector is product differentiation. If UK firms can produce unique products that cannot easily be copied then they will not be in direct competition with the low cost manufacturers in the emerging markets. If they can sell to luxury niche markets and sell to high income households that want unique brands and distinctive products they may establish a Buy British business model that the rest of the world demands.

The UK is a small economy that cannot resist market forces. International competition is fierce and hiding in the EU is not a viable long-term strategy. British firms need to embrace competition and seek to become market leaders. Given that the vast majority of UK jobs are related to retail sales it is in the interests of the Buy British Campaign to support free trade and continue to import low cost clothing from around the world. Britain does have a reasonable manufacturing base but if it is to survive in the future it needs to focus on the top end of the clothing markets and add value where it can.

ⓔ **23/25 marks awarded.** We have placed this answer in mid Level 5 (21–25 marks). The answer meets the Level 5 descriptor, which includes 'well-focused analysis with clear, logical chains of reasoning, and supported evaluation throughout the response'. Two marks have been deducted because the answer lacks an explicit conclusion.

ⓔ Total score: 41/50 marks = Grade A*

Knowledge check answers

Knowledge check answers

1 During and shortly after the 'great recession' in 2008/09, achieving economic recovery (economic growth) and reducing unemployment became the main macroeconomic policy objectives. However, since the change of government in 2010, cutting public expenditure (fiscal austerity) has become an intermediate policy objective in order to 'free resources for the private sector to use' in pursuit of sustainable growth. Controlling inflation and reducing the current account deficit have not been significant objectives in recent years, despite in the latter case the huge size of the deficit.

2 Resource depletion is the consumption of a resource faster than it can be replenished. Environmental degradation is the destruction of ecosystems and the extinction of wildlife, partly as a result of pollution.

3 In circular flow diagrams, money flows result from the fact that for the most part, people receive incomes in the form of money, and likewise their expenditure is in money. In the monetary economy in which we live, real flows of labour and other factor services, and of goods, are paid for using money. In a barter economy, this would not be the case. A monetary economy is more complicated and sophisticated than a barter economy.

4 Microeconomic equilibrium occurs at the level of output *within* a particular market at which the market clears. This occurs at the equilibrium price at which planned demand for the good equals planned supply of the good, ceteris paribus. Macroeconomic equilibrium occurs at the level of *aggregate* output in the *whole* economy, at which the aggregate demand for all goods equals the aggregate supply of all goods $(AD = AS)$.

5 The multiplier measures the relationship between a change in one of the components of aggregate demand, for example investment, and the resulting change in national income. The accelerator measures the reverse relationship — how a change in national income affects the level of investment.

6

7 Money's function as a standard of deferred payment allows people to delay paying for goods or settling a debt, even though goods or services are being provided immediately. Money acts as a standard of deferred payment whenever firms sell goods on credit or draw up contracts specifying a monetary payment due at a later date.

8 People cannot earn interest by holding cash (though they can avoid suffering a capital loss by so doing). Although cash is the most liquid of all assets to hold, it earns no profit.

9 Monetary policy is the part of macroeconomic policy through which the government and the Bank of England attempt to achieve macroeconomic objectives such as control of inflation through the use of monetary policy instruments such as changes in Bank Rate. Fiscal policy is the part of macroeconomic policy through which the government (the Treasury) attempts to achieve macroeconomic objectives such as economic growth through the use of fiscal policy instruments such as changes in tax rates.

10 A budget deficit occurs when the government spends more in its public spending programme than it receives in revenue from taxation and other sources, i.e. when $G > T$. A budget surplus occurs when the government spends less in its public spending programme than it receives in revenue from taxation and other sources, i.e. when $G < T$.

11 A direct tax, such as income tax, is levied directly on those who, in this case, receive the income. People break the law if they fail to pay the tax. A progressive tax is one where the rich pay a larger proportion of their incomes in tax than the poor. In the UK, income tax is both direct and progressive. However, this does not have to be the case. For example, a second income tax, a national insurance contribution (NIC), is direct but regressive.

12 Countries that have found it difficult for their own industries to compete with imports from China have argued that China has been manipulating downwards the exchange rate of the yuan (or renminbi) to give its exports a competitive advantage. They have also argued that China 'dumps' exports such as steel in world markets at prices below the goods' costs of production. Through both these transmission mechanisms the growth of China's trade has 'unfairly' forced competitor industries in other countries into bankruptcy.

13 Not necessarily. Although a balance of payments surplus on current account often results from the price competitiveness and quality competitiveness of a country's exports, it also means that somewhere else in the world one or more other countries suffer deficits, which pose problems, and the surplus may also be inflationary.

Note: Page numbers in **bold** indicate definitions of key terms.

A
absolute advantage **56**
accelerator **18–19**
adaptive expectations theory **30–31**
aggregate demand/aggregate supply analysis 14–17
aggregate demand and economic activity level 19–20
aid **69**
automatic stabilisers **49**

B
balance of payments **8**, 60–63
Bank of England 36, 39–40, 41–42, 43
bank failures 43
Bank Rate **40**
bonds and interest rates 37
broad money **36**
budget balance **48**

C
capital account **60**
capital flows **61–62**, 65
capital ratio **43**
capital–output ratio 18–19
central bank **39–40**
circular flow of income **13–14**
claimant count **25**
closed economy **57**
commercial banks **37–38**
comparative advantage **56**
consumer prices index (CPI) **28**
cost-push inflation **29–30**
credit creation 39
currency union **65–66**
current account **60**, 61, 62, 63, 64
customs union **58**
cyclical budget deficit **48**
cyclical unemployment **26–27**

D
debt **37**
deflation **28**, 31, 62
deindustrialisation **55**
demand-pull inflation **29**
devaluation **62**
development 66–69
direct tax **47**, 48
disinflation **28**

E
economic cycle **16**, 24–25, 48
economic development **10**
economic growth **8**, 16, 22–24
  barriers to 67–68
  factors affecting 67
  indicators of 10
  policies to promote 68
  role of aid and trade 69
  supply-side policies 50
  vs. development 66
economic performance 7, 22–35
economic shock **17**, 25
economic welfare **10–11**
equilibrium national income **15**
equity 37
European Union (EU) **58**
eurozone **65–66**
exchange rate **8, 11**
  determination 63–64
  effect of changes in 40–41
  fixed vs. floating 65
  government intervention 64–65
expenditure-reducing policy **62**
expenditure-switching policy **62**
exports **14**
export subsidies **58**

F
financial account **60**
financial markets **36–37**
fiscal policy **19**, 45–49
fixed exchange rate systems 65
floating exchange rate systems 63–64, 65

D
foreign direct investment (FDI) **59**
foreign exchange (FX) markets **36**
free-market supply-side policies 52
frictional unemployment **25**
full employment **8**, 9, 21, 27

G
globalisation **54–56**
government spending **14**, 17, 19, 45, 46–47, 48
  demand-pull inflation 29
  fiscal policy 45, 46–47, 48
  multiplier process 19–20
  supply-side policies 52–53
gross domestic product (GDP) **13**
gross national income (GNI) 10, 67

H
human capital **55**
Human Development Index (HDI) **67**

I
imports **14**
index numbers **9–10**
indirect tax **47**
inflation **8**, 28–34, 40, 41
infrastructure **55**
injections **14**
interest rates and bonds 37
international trade 56–59
investment **14**
  accelerator theory 18–19
  and development 67, 68
  flows between countries 61–62
  vs. savings 18
investment banks **37**
involuntary unemployment **25**

K
Keynesian *AS* curve 20–21

L
Labour Force Survey (LFS) **25**
less-developed countries **55–56**
  main characteristics of 66–67